The Marathon Chef Michel Roux Jr

The Marathon Chef Michel Roux Jr
Food for Getting Fit

Photography by Tara Fisher

WEIDENFELD & NICOLSON

'People often ask me why I run. The simple answer is it makes me hungry!'

contents

running a marathon

I love good food but I also love to be fit, and running marathons has become a passion. I've always liked running. I was one of the few who enjoyed cross-country races at school and when I started in the restaurant business I went jogging to work off some of the stress and tension. Running makes me feel wonderful, elated. After about 45 minutes you get a buzz and even a second wind.

My interest in marathon running began ten years ago. I gave up smoking and three months later I found I had gained 12 kilos. That was when I decided to get serious about being fit. I developed a regular routine and started to run several times a week. Soon I was losing weight – while still enjoying my food – and I found I was calmer and less stressed. The migraines I had suffered from for years disappeared.

I was enjoying running so much I wanted to have a goal so I entered for the London Marathon. The hard work really began and I embarked on a proper training programme. My first marathon was amazing. I set myself a target of coming in under four hours – in fact I finished in 3 hours 27 minutes, which is pretty good going for a first-timer. I felt great afterwards and the next day I was back at work as usual. Obviously I did have aches and pains – the first time was the worst – but they are not unbearable and you have such an incredible feeling of achievement. Since then I have run marathons in London (four times), New York, Monaco, Bordeaux and Tromsø in Norway. I hope to do many more.

Over the years I have thought a great deal about the best way to eat while training, and I've worked out a healthy eating pattern that suits my life and makes me feel good. I'm a chef. I work with food all day and every day and

I love to eat well. Fortunately, I've found that you can enjoy the best food and stay fit and lean by just a little adjustment. I have learned to tailor delicious food combinations to maximize my energy and stamina, and many of these recipes are now regulars at Le Gavroche – that tells you how good they are.

Even when I'm not in training I run two or three times a week for 45 minutes. When I'm preparing for a marathon it's more, and I do one long-distance run of at least two hours every week. I jog or walk for five or ten minutes, do some stretching exercises so I don't damage cold muscles, then off I go on my run. Afterwards I usually cool down with a few more stretches on all the major muscles, holding them for 30 to 60 seconds – some experts say this is even more important than warming up beforehand.

Afternoon is my time for running. I don't like to run first thing in the morning. A run in the afternoon fits in with my day and my body is warmed up and ready. You may think – and I did at first – that you don't have time to run. You're too busy. But I find the time I spend running is by no means wasted. It's a great opportunity to think through problems, make plans and mull things over without the distractions of phone calls and other people. I can think clearly and I come back refreshed and relaxed. And when I'm

exercising I manage the rest of my time better and I'm generally more efficient, so there's no question of running causing me to neglect my work. There are days when I wonder why I'm doing this to myself – especially when it's wet and windy – but once I get warmed up I forget my reluctance and enjoy myself.

I've lost weight through running. I also get hungrier, but strangely enough it's made me less tempted to eat heavy, fatty foods. Training seems to make my body want the right things. I haven't turned my back on foods such as red

meat, cheese and butter – I enjoy them too much and would never contem-
plate giving up such tasty, satisfying food – but I don't eat them as often as I
used to.

You don't have to run fast or set personal best times – or enter a marathon
– for running to be beneficial. Run at your own pace, set your own goals. If
you want to compete with other runners, start with short races and fun runs.
Once you've taken that initial step, the pleasures of running are not far away.
I always say that anyone can complete a marathon. The most difficult part is
tackling it in your mind

What running does for you Experts now agree that vigorous exercise helps
you deal with stress, lifts depression and generally makes you feel a whole lot
better. Regular runners have higher energy levels than non-runners. Here's
what regular running – even if you don't aspire to a marathon – can do for
you. Running teaches you discipline and improves your time management.
It relieves tension and lessens stress, lifts depression, and cures problems such
as headaches and migraines. It also keeps your heart and lungs in good
condition, increases your feeling of well-being and makes you feel more
cheerful. Running helps you to sleep better, speeds weight loss and helps to
keep blood pressure down. And it encourages good eating habits – when
you're running regularly your body seems to want the right foods

Le Gavroche The London restaurant Le Gavroche was opened by the Roux
brothers, Albert and Michel, in 1967. With its superb classical French food
and the highest standards of cooking and service, it quickly became legendary
and remains so to this day. Michel Roux Jr trained as a chef with Maître
Patissier Hellegouarche in Paris and Alain Chapel at Mionay, Lyon, and took
over the running of Le Gavroche from his father in 1994. Michel's style is
modern French – classic French dishes with a light, fresh, healthy approach,
drawing on influences and flavours from Asia and the Mediterranean.

Preparation

If, like me, you enjoy running and you're fit and healthy you could think about running a marathon. But if you're serious about long-distance running, hours of training must be done. This is the hard part. If you have trained properly, the race is there to be enjoyed. Any cheating and your body will soon let you know. The first month or so of training is fine, but by the seventh or eighth week you just want the date to arrive so you can get it over with. You need to start training for a marathon at least three months before the event, assuming you already have a good level of fitness. Run several times a week for 45 minutes or so and do one longer run of two hours or more. Don't forget your stretches and do some core strength exercises to improve your stability. Don't overdo it though – runners need to be lean. Bulky heavy muscles will only slow you down.

Don't suddenly increase the distance you run. This can lead to injury and fatigue. Increase the length of your long run gradually and be sure to rest well between runs.

As the date gets nearer, keep up your training rigorously. Do your last big run two weeks before – try for a minimum half distance or as much as three-quarters – then taper down your training. The Sunday before the race, go for an hour's run, then reduce to shorter runs each day and allow yourself two whole days off running before the race. For a Sunday run I usually work Friday and rest on Saturday to prepare for the big day. Running magazines usually publish training schedules, which can be very useful to follow.

Eating well I like to eat good-quality, seasonal foods, prepared simply but well. There's no need to suffer. You can be slim and fit and still enjoy your food – everything in moderation is the key. I like natural products. I never eat 'light' versions of foods. If you love butter and cream, eat the proper stuff, but not too often. It's far better to have some delicious top-quality butter or cream once in a while rather than lots of tasteless low-fat spread or cream.

In general, though, I avoid butter in cooking and use olive oil, but not too much. Instead of cooking vegetables in butter or oil, use a non-stick pan and sprinkle a little good oil on to your food before serving so you get the maximum flavour.

Ready meals are a pet hate of mine. They are full of additives that do nothing for taste, let alone health. Good, natural tasty food that gives you pleasure is never going to make you put on the kilos. The feel-good factor means you are less inclined to binge on something silly like cheap cakes or confectionery.

I like foods in their proper season. I don't want to eat strawberries at Christmas. I like them in the summer on a long June evening. I look forward to eating asparagus in May, wild salmon in July, blackberries in September. That is when they are at their best, full of flavour and with peak nutritional value since they have more chance of having been picked ripe and not brought from the other side of the world. When raw ingredients are good there is no need to do much to them. They are delicious served as simply as possible. In France there is more emphasis on seasonal local produce, even in supermarkets. There is more of a market culture there, but in recent years interest in local farmers' markets and fresh local produce has grown in the UK, and that can only be good for our eating habits.

Enjoying good food and good wine is not elitist or snobbish. It just makes sense. Look for the best-quality, freshest produce you can afford – whether you're buying a joint of meat, a loaf of bread or a bag of carrots – and your cooking will benefit.

I confess that I do like sweet things – more as I get older! And when I'm running a lot my body craves that glucose fix. Obviously you mustn't overdo it, but a sweet treat after a long run or a workout does you no harm. The puddings in this book contain lots of fruit and not too much fat or sugar. I like chocolate, too, but only the best. I hate cheap chocolate and sweets and I just don't see the point of eating them.

Wine is fine – but don't forget the water I do drink but only good wine. Even the night before a marathon a glass or two of red wine is fine. I drink water or sports drinks while running. Lucozade works for me and helps to replace the minerals I lose while running. While on the subject of drink, I believe that water is life. No liquid is more important for your body or a better thirst quencher than pure water. Working in a hot kitchen, I drink at least 10 glasses a day and if in training three or four litres is not unusual. Beer is not a good substitute, nor is tea or coffee. They are all diuretics and dry you out more than they hydrate you.

What to eat, when

You don't have to be draconian with your diet when training for long-distance running. Just more aware. I am a strong believer in listening to your body and letting it tell you what it needs. And food that is attractive and tastes good satisfies the senses as well as nutritional needs.

When I'm training for a marathon I eat plenty of fruit and vegetables. I don't usually feel like eating meat – it's too heavy. If I'm going to run in the afternoon I have a late breakfast of cereal, juice and fruit, with perhaps some bread and butter and coffee. It's bad to run on an empty tum. You need some ballast. After the run I might treat myself to a delicious salad dish, such as an endive and poached egg salad with some bread – and a little good chocolate to follow. Then vegetables and perhaps pasta or rice for dinner. I might have some fruit after dinner or a pudding made with muscovado, not white, sugar. Muscovado has a better flavour and you need less of it.

Eating out Many people say they find it difficult to stick to their regime when they go out to a restaurant or a party and end up eating and drinking too much. It shouldn't be that difficult. I eat at Le Gavroche twice a day, five times a week and always go out to eat at least once on my days off. Not only that, but if Le Gavroche can offer dishes on the menu that are not going to make you feel like a sumo wrestler, then there are no excuses. First step is to stop drinking spirits, before and after a meal. If you do drink them while training, you will ache like hell the following day. I find it easier to say no from the outset rather than 'Oh, just one glass won't hurt.' Saying no is not a sign of weakness but quite the opposite. It shows strength of character and willpower. If you are going to drink, drink wine and make sure it is good. Why bother if it is not is my way of looking at it. And drink water, plenty of it. It'll keep you from drinking too much alcohol.

When eating out, look at the menu and avoid dishes that are obviously going to be heavy, described with words like 'braised', 'stew' and 'creams'.

Keep up the carbs We all need to eat carbohydrates for energy. Carbohydrate is stored in the muscles and liver as glycogen. We can only store fairly limited amounts so need to keep carbohydrate levels topped up. Low levels of glycogen will mean you get tired quickly and cannot perform at your best. High levels of glycogen help you work and train hard. Glycogen levels are depleted by exercise – that's why it's important to eat after a run.

What I eat My diet is high in carbohydrates. This has never been a problem for me because I love pastas and breads. I don't believe that bread, pasta or potatoes actually make you fat. It is what you put on them. Unrefined carbohydrates, such as wholegrain cereals and flours, brown rice, potatoes, pulses, carrots and other root vegetables, are much better for you than the refined starches found in processed cereals, white flour, cakes and biscuits. Refined starch gives you a speedy, short-term boost but doesn't sustain energy long term. Unrefined carbohydrate is absorbed more slowly by the body and so releases energy gradually and keeps you going longer.

The basic rule of eating high-carbohydrate food in the days leading up to a race is well known. But too many novices pig out on a big bowl of spaghetti carbonara or baked potato with sour cream and cheese the night before, only to feel dreadful and heavy legged the following morning. I like to stock up on carbohydrates in the week before the race and stick to lighter foods for the last couple of days. And although we need fats to assimilate some vital minerals and vitamins, it is best to avoid copious amounts the night before running a marathon.

Muscles need protein to grow and recover from exercise, but I think that unless you are into bodybuilding (which I am not) vitamin C is probably more important for runners. Not only does it ward off colds, which can severely hamper your training schedule and even force you to withdraw from an event, but it also helps to flush out the toxins given out by muscles when exercising. The body does not retain vitamin C and so it must be consumed daily. Fresh fruit juices are an easy source, but steer clear of reconstituted fruit drinks which are full of artificial sweeteners and additives. Zinc and copper are also important. Zinc is found in abundance in oysters as well as in beans and whole grains. Nuts, seafood and beans contain copper as does chocolate – my favourite source. Vitamin E is another powerful antioxidant that the body can never get enough of. It's found in almonds, pumpkin seeds and peanut butter.

Fats can be good for you Most diets urge you to restrict fats and this is right if you lead a sedentary life. But an intake of less than 20 per cent fat is not good for endurance runners or people who take vigorous exercise regularly. The ideal body fat percentage for athletes is 6–15 per cent for males and 12–18 per cent for females. You need an intake of 30 per cent fat if you are training for a marathon. Not only will you not gain any weight but you will also be able to eat some really tasty foods. Be careful though – eat good-quality vegetable and animal fats, not rubbish.

Enjoy eating cheese. Although it is high fat, cheese is not as bad for you as was once thought. Because of the high calcium content of cheese much of the fat is not absorbed by the body. What's more, it tastes great, particularly the unpasteurized farmhouse varieties.

Energy foods If there is one thing every runner knows it is that they should eat plenty of carbo-hydrates. But not all carbs are equal. Choose your carbohydrate foods wisely and they could improve your energy levels and concentration, stop you feeling hungry all the time, and even reduce your sugar cravings.

The secret of choosing the right carbohydrates is to check the glycaemic index, which tells you how quickly carbohydrates are converted to sugar and absorbed by the blood. The index measures the amount by which 50 grams of a particular carbohydrate raises your blood sugar in the two-hour period after it is eaten, compared with 50 grams of sugar, which has a glycaemic index, or GI, of 100. Fast-digesting carbohydrates have a high GI (above 70), medium-digesting carbs have a GI of 55 to 70 and slow-digesting carbs have a GI of less than 55.

High GI foods are absorbed quickly and are best eaten during or shortly before a run, since they provide easily accessible energy for your muscles. They're also useful straight afterwards because they help to replenish your depleted carb stores quickly. But if you eat lots of high GI foods at other times you will find yourself feeling hungry again soon after eating. High GI foods can also raise your blood-sugar levels, making you feel sleepy after eating, and cause an excessive surge of insulin in the blood, which leaves you feeling shaky and irritable.

Balancing your carbohydrates

The bulk of your daily carbohydrate intake should be made up of low and medium GI foods, which help to keep blood-sugar levels stable. A meal of medium GI foods eaten two or three hours before a run can delay fatigue by supplying energy to the muscles during exercise. After your run, a meal of medium and high GI foods helps you recover your energy. Here are some examples of foods in all three GI groups.

LOW GI FOODS
eat plenty of these
porridge
high-fibre cereals
barley
basmati rice
pumpernickel bread
cauliflower
broccoli
cabbage
sprouts
peas
peaches
pears
apples
nectarines
grapes
sultanas
apricots
cherries
kiwis
plums
gooseberries
oranges
lemons
grapefruit
butter and broad beans
lentils
chickpeas
split peas

MEDIUM GI FOODS
eat plenty of these
muesli (without sugar)
semolina
bran cereal with fruit
brown/wild rice
new potatoes with skin
pasta
sweetcorn
couscous
rye bread
bran muffins
oatmeal/bran crumpets
beetroot
spinach
banana
lychees
mangoes
pineapple
melon
raisins
dates
honey
sugar (don't have more
than 4–6 tsp a day)

HIGH GI FOODS
go easy with these
shredded wheat cereal
puffed wheat cereal
white rice
potatoes
wholewheat/brown
bread or rolls
pitta bread
bagels
carrots
pumpkin
butternut squash
parsnips
watermelon

limit these refined carbs
corn flakes
puffed rice cereal
instant oat cereal
mashed potato
fried chips and crisps
white bread and rolls
rice cakes
scones
crumpets
cakes

The night before

The night before running a marathon, eat something light but nourishing – fish and vegetables are my choice. All major marathons hold what is often called a 'Pasta Party' the night before the event. This may be in a local Italian trattoria or under a marquee with big bubbling vats of spaghetti to feed the masses. They are fun and you do get to meet like-minded people, but generally I prefer my own menu. If you are eating a big bowl of pasta the night before because you need to load up on carbohydrates, you have left it too late. Too many carbohydrates can leave you bloated and deficient in other nutrients that are equally important when running long distances. If you have not trained for the event properly, last-minute exertion is too late. Likewise with the diet. I load up on carbohydrates three to four days prior to running a race, then relax the night before, glad that the tedium of training is over. I feel confident of my preparation, yet filled with expectation

Far more important in my view is what you avoid the night before, rather than what you eat. I try to have a normal diet without pigging out. Play safe. No shellfish. Any drastic change of habit could throw your body and metabolism out of balance, so now is the not the time to experiment. Whether you go out for dinner or eat at home, your meal should be light but satisfying, so fish is a good option; spicy curry is not!

A glass or two of wine, preferably red, not only helps the digestion but also relaxes the mind, which helps you to get a good night's sleep and be ready for an early start the next day. Don't be tempted to drink more – alcohol dries out the body and running any distance, even for the bus, with a hangover is not much fun.

Use a little common sense and think before you order or prepare your meal. I tend to eat early then relax in front of television or read a book. A snack of biscuits or a piece of good chocolate an hour before bed helps you sleep well and ensures that your glycogen levels are not depleted when you wake up the next morning.

Breakfast is a personal matter. What works for one runner may not be ideal for another. I always have a double-strength coffee and buttered toast with jam before a marathon, but I know some runners who just can't face any solids. Others sit down to boiled eggs! Eat what you feel comfortable with and trial and error will tell you what works for you.

During the race Have a snack such as a cereal bar half an hour before the race starts. And keep up your fluid intake. The rule is to drink before you feel thirsty – if you're thirsty your body is already dehydrated which won't help you during the race. So-called feeding stations where you can get drinks are positioned along the course (at the Paris Marathon you get food too) so take advantage of these. Water is fine for the early stages, but after 90 minutes you will need sports beverages to replenish your body. You can also ask friends to position themselves along the way with fruit or snacks if you need them. At the Médoc Marathon in France, feeding stations hand out not only glasses of wine but also grilled steaks and oysters! Many runners don't manage to reach the finish line of that race. As a rule, though, steer clear of alcohol as well as drinks containing caffeine such as tea, coffee and fizzy drinks.

Next day Elation, a sense of achievement – and aching feet and legs. But I've never felt the pain to be unbearable and I've never missed a day's work because of a marathon. Have something to eat soon after finishing the race, ideally within 15 minutes, and have a good stretch. The experts say that eating carbohydrates soon after rigorous, long-duration exercise such as a marathon helps to avoid muscle fatigue the next day.

Don't rush for the champagne bottle. Alcohol after all that exercise will dehydrate you and make you ache more the next day. I normally put my feet up for the rest of the day or perhaps take a soak in a hot tub or Jacuzzi. I feel I deserve a rest so I don't run for a few days. Then I begin some exercise, go for a short run – and start thinking about the next marathon.

A week's training menu

All the recipes for the following menus are contained in the book. They're delicious – and healthy. Cook them and enjoy yourself.

SUNDAY
Breakfast
Kedgeree

Lunch
Watercress soup

Wholemeal bread

Dinner
Spaghetti with razor clams, parsley and garlic

Warm chocolate and honey cake with dried fruit salad

MONDAY
Breakfast
Crumpets

Blueberry banana smoothie

Lunch
Endive and poached egg salad with red onions and dry-cured bacon

Soft rye bread buns

Dinner
Boiled lamb shanks with star anise broth, potatoes and turnips

Warm spicy stir-fried fruits

TUESDAY
Breakfast
Cereal

Charentais melon spiced with ginger and basil

Lunch
Butter beans with chorizo and tomato

Dinner
Watercress and pear salad

Stuffed sea bass with Creole rice

Chocolate-dipped fruits

WEDNESDAY
Breakfast
Truffled scrambled eggs

Lunch
Tunisian grilled vegetable salad

Fougasse bread with olives

Dinner
Tagliatelle with green olive paste and Bayonne ham

Poached plums in red wine with toasted spiced bread croutons

THURSDAY
Breakfast
Toasted rye buns with poached eggs, baby spinach and crispy bacon

Lunch
Squash and prawn soup with pumpkin seed biscuits

Pastilla of apples and prunes with salted caramel sauce

Dinner
Chicken supreme with pearl barley broth

Oriental summer salad

FRIDAY
Breakfast
Toast with almond and honey spread or praline and chocolate spread

White peach and almond drink

Lunch
Baked ham and spinach pancakes with a green salad

Dinner
French bean and wet walnut salad

Calves' liver with wild mushrooms and sweet and sour onion, with a jacket potato

Roast figs in vine leaves

SATURDAY
Breakfast
Pikelets

Strawberries and orange with basil

Watermelon and papaya wake-up juice

Lunch
Grilled tiger prawns with cucumber salad and pistachio yogurt dressing

Black pepper bap

Dinner
Chestnut and apple soup with rosemary

Goat's cheese bread

Roast gilt-head bream with mustard and parsley, and wholewheat pasta

Banana soufflé with crumble topping

Marathons to aspire to

There's a marathon happening somewhere in the world every month of the year. They include city marathons, gruelling races over rugged landscapes, races by the sea and through deserts. In short – something for everyone.

JANUARY

Lantau Mountain Marathon
Lantau, China
(includes some testing climbs)

Trinidad Marathon
Port of Spain, Trinidad and Tobago

Walt Disney World Marathon
Orlando, Florida
(flat course passes through theme parks)

FEBRUARY

Sahara Marathon
L'Ayoun, Algeria
(gruelling desert course)

Buller Marathon
Westport, New Zealand
(New Zealand's most scenic course)

MARCH

Six Foot Track (Ultra) Marathon
Sydney, Australia
(Australia's largest off-road marathon – 46km trail through the Blue Mountains National Park)

City of Los Angeles Marathon
Los Angeles, USA
(entertainment centres along the course help keep you cheerful)

Roma Marathon
Rome, Italy
(course passes many of the city's major tourist attractions)

Antarctica Marathon
Antarctica
(toughest of them all)

Thailand Temple Run
Thailand
(passes through picturesque country with 100 temples; started in 2002)

APRIL

Paris International Marathon
Paris, France

London Marathon
London, UK
(one of the biggest; great crowds, great atmosphere)

Leipzig Marathon
Leipzig, Germany

Hamburg Hanse-Marathon
Hamburg, Germany

Boston Marathon
Boston USA
(world's oldest marathon; strict qualifying standards)

Rotterdam Marathon
Netherlands
(one of the flattest and fastest courses)

Two Oceans Marathon
Cape Town, South Africa
(one of the most scenic marathons)

Big Sur Marathon
California, USA
(largest rural marathon in the world, through stunning scenery)

North Pole Marathon
North Pole Base Camp
Russian Federation
(running on Arctic ice floes)

Madrid Marathon
Madrid, Spain

MAY

Great Wall Marathon
Beijing, China
(part of the course is on the Wall; 3,700 steps to climb)

Adidas Vancouver International Marathon
Vancouver, Canada

Neolithic Marathon
Avebury, UK
(finishes at the historic site of Stonehenge)

Gutsmuths Rennsteiglauf
GutsMuth, Germany

Internationale Twente Marathon
Enschede, Netherlands

JUNE

Edge to Edge Marathon
Ucluelet, Canada

Marathon de la baie du Mont St Michel
Cancale, France

Stockholm Marathon
Sweden
(the biggest sporting event in Sweden)

Midnight Sun Marathon
Tromsø, Norway
(run in broad daylight in the middle of the night)

Comrades Marathon
South Africa
(course from Durban to Pietermaritzburg)

Lewa Safaricom Marathon
Kenya
(run with Masai tribespeople)

JULY

Yukon River Trail Marathon
Whitehorse, Canada

AUGUST

Nachtmarathon
Marburg, Germany
(race starts at 7 in the evening)

Helsinki City Marathon
Helsinki, Finland

Reykjavik Marathon
Reykjavik, Iceland
(perfect running temperatures and crystal-clean air)

Medvinds Marathon
Copenhagen, Denmark

SEPTEMBER

Usedom Marathon
Wogast, Germany

Marathon du Médoc
Médoc, France
(wine and good food served at feeding stations)

Mergelland Marathon
Meerssen, Netherlands

Moscow International Peace Marathon
Moscow, Russia

Trondheim Marathon
Trondheim,

Berlin Marathon
Berlin, Germany

Jungfrau Marathon
Switzerland
(a mountain marathon and one of the most beautiful)

OCTOBER

Ford Koeln (Cologne) Marathon
Cologne, Germany

Royal Victoria Marathon
Vancouver Island, Canada

Eindhoven Marathon
Eindhoven, Netherlands

Melbourne Marathon
Melbourne, Australia

Frankfurt Marathon
Frankfurt, Germany
(the oldest marathon in Germany)

Delta Lloyd Amsterdam Marathon
Amsterdam, Netherlands

Casino Niagara International Marathon
Niagara Falls, Canada

Dublin Marathon
Dublin, Ireland

La Salle Bank Chicago Marathon
Chicago, USA
(takes in the sights of Chicago)

Dead Sea Marathon
Jordan
(course goes down to the lowest point on earth)

NOVEMBER

Tokyo International Women's Marathon
Tokyo, Japan

New York City Marathon
New York, USA
(one of the world's favourites)

Philadelphia Marathon
Philadelphia, USA

Monaco Marathon
Monte Carlo

DECEMBER

Pending Kenyatta International Marathon
Nyeri, Kenya

California International Marathon
Sacramento, USA

Honolulu Marathon
Hawaii
(starts at 5am; wonderful views of the Pacific at sunrise)

Reggae Marathon
Jamaica
(run to reggae music)

breakfast

Strawberries and Orange with Basil

SERVES 4

200g strawberries

10 basil leaves, plus some for decoration

4 oranges

light muscovado sugar to taste

Wash the strawberries in cold water, drain and hull. If the berries are large, cut them into bite-size pieces.

Using a small, sharp knife, peel the oranges, removing all the pith. Cut them into segments, leaving behind the pithy membrane between each segment. Squeeze the membrane to extract any juice. Mix the oranges and strawberries together. Wash the basil leaves, cut them into strips and add them to the fruit. Spoon the fruit into little bowls, sprinkle with sugar to taste and decorate with a basil leaf and a thin slice of orange.

Pikelets

Of Welsh origin, these pikelets are delicious for breakfast with home-made preserves and a good Brittany salted butter.

MAKES 10–12

320g self-raising flour

80g caster sugar

1 large egg

milk

90g unsalted butter

1 tsp white wine vinegar

¼ tsp bicarbonate of soda

Sift the flour and sugar into a bowl. Add the egg and enough milk to make a thick batter, whisking well to avoid lumps. Melt the butter, add the vinegar and bicarbonate of soda and mix into the batter. Drop a few spoonfuls of batter on to a hot, lightly greased frying pan – use crumpet rings if you want a perfect shape. Cook until bubbles appear on the surface and the bottoms are browned. Flip over and cook the other side. Repeat until all the batter is used up. Store the pikelets in the refrigerator and toast when you want them or eat immediately, hot from the pan.

You can make pikelets with spelt flour or unbleached stoneground flour – good for your complex carbohydrate intake but slightly heavier to eat.

Watermelon and Papaya Wake-Up Juice

SERVES 6

300g very ripe watermelon, skin removed

1 ripe papaya, peeled and de-seeded

juice of 1 lime

3 ice cubes

1 tbsp sugar (optional)

Cut the watermelon into chunks and put it in a blender with the lime juice, papaya and ice cubes. Blend until smooth and add a little sugar to taste.

Crumpets

MAKES 16–18

350g strong bread flour

a pinch of salt

1 tsp caster sugar

25g fresh yeast

450ml milk

2 large eggs

Mix the flour, salt and sugar together in a bowl. Melt the yeast in the warmed milk and pour this and the beaten eggs into the flour mix. Whisk the batter well to get rid of any lumps, then beat with a spatula for at least 5 minutes. Cover with a cloth and leave to rest for 1 hour. Cook in the same way as the pikelets on page 28 but use crumpet rings or a blini pan.

Great eaten just out of the pan or toasted. These crumpets are perfect for breakfast or delicious with cured ham or salt beef as a hot open sandwich. The recipe also works with wholemeal or stoneground spelt flour.

Buckwheat and Potato Pancakes

MAKES 10–12

200g cooked boiled potato

100g buckwheat flour

1 egg

200ml milk

1tsp baking power

salt, pepper, nutmeg

olive oil

Pass the boiled potatoes through a ricer or coarse sieve. Whisk the flour, egg, milk, baking powder and seasoning together in a bowl and add the potato. Cover and leave to rest for 10 minutes.

Preheat the oven to 190°C/gas mark 5. Heat a little blini pan measuring about 8cm across x 1.5cm deep, add a little olive oil and drop in a few spoonfuls of the mixture. Each pancake should be about 6mm thick. Cook over a medium heat until the mixture bubbles at the sides, then put the pan in the oven for 4 minutes to set the pancake. Remove from the oven and use a pallet knife to turn the pancake over to cook on the other side, adding a drop of oil if necessary. Repeat until all the mixture is used up. If you don't have blini pans, use an ordinary frying pan.

Delicious as a savoury breakfast with eggs or black pudding or eaten the American way with a good-quality maple syrup.

To make this pancake lighter, separate the egg, add an extra egg white, whisk both until stiff and fold into the mix at the end.

Truffled Scrambled Eggs

This has to be the best way to eat scrambled eggs ever. Too rich to eat before a run, the promise of a breakfast like this is a great incentive to get you over the line. My personal preference is for perfectly ripe black Périgord truffles from France, *Tuber melanosporum*, which are at their best from the end of December to February. You can also use white truffles from Piedmont in Italy, *Tuber magnatum*, but I wouldn't consider using any other variety. By mixing with a wooden spatula instead of a whisk and adding seasoning at the end as described below, you end up with larger softer lumps in your scrambled eggs, especially if you like them runny. Also delicious with duck eggs or gull eggs.

SERVES 4

8 fresh organic free-range eggs
1 or 2 truffles, about 80g
4 tbsp double cream
salt, pepper
1 tbsp butter

Put the eggs and truffles together in an airtight container and refrigerate for 3–5 days before you use them. Because the shells are porous the eggs soak up the scent given off by the truffles.

Smear the bottom of a thick copper-lined pan with the butter and break in the eggs. Set the pan over a medium heat and start mixing the eggs with a wooden spatula. Keep working the mixture and scraping the pan continuously until the scrambled eggs are cooked as you like, then season and halt the cooking process by adding the cream. Slice the truffles thinly and sprinkle on top of the eggs. Serve immediately.

I used to cook this dish for breakfast when doing my military service at the Palais de l'Elysée. It was a favourite of President François Mitterand.

Toasted Rye Buns with Poached Eggs, Baby Spinach and Crispy Bacon

SERVES 4

4 large organic eggs

8 slices of organic ventreche, pancetta or dry cure streaky bacon, very thinly sliced

4 rye buns (see page 49)

200g baby spinach

1 tsp white wine vinegar

salt, pepper

Put a litre of water into a pan with the vinegar and bring to a rolling boil. Crack the eggs into small ramekins and gently slide each egg into the water. Turn the heat down to a gentle simmer and poach the eggs for 3–4 minutes, depending on how runny you like them. Using a slotted spoon, remove the eggs from the water and trim the edges.

Meanwhile, grill the bacon until crispy over a tray to collect the fat. Halve and toast the rye buns. Wash and dry the spinach. For each bun, place some spinach leaves on the bottom half and pour on some fat and juice from the bacon. Season with freshly ground pepper, add an egg and season with salt and more pepper. Lay two slices of bacon over the egg and top with the other half of the bun.

Charentais Melon Spiced with Ginger and Basil

Ginger gives a great kick to food and drinks. I like to think that it also gives me that extra bit of kick that's needed in the final stretch of a race. This wonderful root aids digestion, stimulates the heart and is a strong antioxidant and an anti-inflammatory. One of my favourite after-dinner teas is made by pouring boiling water over thinly sliced fresh ginger and a crushed lemon grass stem and leaving it to steep for 5 minutes. Perfect after a heavy meal.

SERVES 6

2 ripe Charentais melons

20–30g fresh ginger, peeled and diced

10 basil leaves

6 ice cubes

white pepper

Cut the melon into eight and remove the seeds and skin. Put the melon into a blender with the ice, basil leaves and ginger. Blend until smooth and pass through a coarse sieve if necessary. Add white pepper to taste.

White Peach and Almond Drink

SERVES 4

4 ripe peaches

sugar (optional)

Wash the peaches in cold water, cut in half and remove the stones. Place the peach stones on a hard flat surface and, using a mallet or back of a heavy knife, crack each one open to extract the kernel. These taste like bitter almonds and give a delicious finish to the peach drink.

Put the peach halves and kernels in a blender and add sugar to taste – if the peaches are perfectly ripe they won't need any. Blend the fruit and kernels until smooth and pass through a coarse sieve if necessary. Decorate each glass with a slice of peach and an almond tuile (see page 38).

Blueberry Banana Smoothie

SERVES 6

3 ripe bananas

250g blueberries

200ml milk

2 tbsp maple syrup

Peel and chop the bananas and put them in a blender with the rest of the ingredients – keep some blueberries to decorate each serving. Blend until smooth. Top each glassful with a few blueberries and perhaps some banana crisps made the day before.

For banana crisps, peel a hard, underripe banana and slice it as thinly as possible lengthways. Put the slices on a non-stick baking mat, dust with icing sugar and dry out in a low oven, 110°C/gas mark ½, until brown and crisp. The crisps keep in an airtight container for a couple of days.

Cherry Ripple with Cinnamon

Cherries contain a high level of vitamin C and bioflavonoids, which makes them a good antioxidant as well as tasting great. Juices like this are always best freshly made, but I would not recommend them before a run – acid build-up in the stomach could give you heartburn.

SERVES 4

250g black cherries

250g white cherries

1 Granny Smith apple

juice of 1 lemon

2 tsp light demerara sugar

2 tsp ground cinnamon and 4 cinnamon quills to finish

Use a centrifugal juice extractor, if you have one, for this recipe, but a blender works almost as well.

Wash the cherries and remove the stalks and stones. Peel the apple and cut it in half. Put the white cherries, half an apple and half the lemon juice in the blender with a teaspoon of sugar and a little water if needed and blend until smooth. Press through a coarse sieve. Repeat the process with the black cherries and the remaining apple, lemon juice and sugar. Gently pour some of each juice simultaneously into tall glasses. Finish with a sprinkling of ground cinnamon and decorate with a cinnamon quill.

Almond Tuiles

MAKES 20–30
80g butter, softened
120g icing sugar
3 egg whites
1 tsp vanilla essence
75g plain flour
50g flaked almonds

Preheat the oven to 220°C/gas mark 7. Cream the soft butter and sugar. Gradually whisk in the egg whites and vanilla essence, then fold in the sifted flour. Leave to rest for 10 minutes.

Using a piping bag, pipe round or long shapes on to a non-stick baking mat and sprinkle with flaked almonds. Put in the hot oven and cook for about 10 minutes until light brown and set. Remove from the oven and roll each tuile around a rolling pin or into a cup to make the desired shape.

Almond and Honey Spread

Honey and almonds help the body fight infections by boosting the immune system. Almonds are also rich in vital vitamins and minerals and high in protein. This makes a healthy, delicious spread for breakfast toast.

120g good-quality chopped or whole blanched almonds
250ml water
3 tbsp clear honey

Put all the ingredients in a blender and mix until smooth. If you want a crunchy finish, keep a few almonds back and add them towards the end of the processing. You could also add a couple of drops of vanilla or almond essence. Scrape the mixture into an airtight container such as a clean jam jar and refrigerate. It keeps for several weeks.

Banana, Orange and Mixed Spice Jam

MAKES ONE LARGE JAR
5 bananas
juice of 1 lemon
juice of 1 orange
50g light muscovado sugar
a pinch of ground mixed spice
1 vanilla pod, scraped

Put the orange and lemon juice in a pan, add the sugar and bring to the boil. Simmer for 3 minutes and add the sliced bananas, mixed spice and the seeds from the vanilla pod. Simmer for another 10–12 minutes while breaking up the bananas with a fork. Pour the boiling hot jam into a clean glass jar and seal. Keep refrigerated and eat within two weeks.

Praline and Chocolate Spread

100g hazelnuts, skinned
100g almonds, blanched
160g extra-bitter dark chocolate, 70% cocoa solids
80g light muscovado sugar
160ml water

Roast the nuts on a baking tray at 180°C/gas mark 4 until they turn a light golden colour. Chop the chocolate into pieces and gently melt in a double boiler.

To make the praline, put the sugar in a saucepan with 50ml of water. Place over a high heat, stirring occasionally until the sugar has totally dissolved, then cook until thick and caramelized. Add the nuts, cook for 2 minutes, then add the remaining water. Stir well, bring back to the boil for 2 minutes and then take the pan off the heat and leave to cool slightly.

Pour the praline mixture, roasted nuts and melted chocolate into a blender and mix until smooth. Put in an airtight container such as a jam jar and store in the refrigerator. Keeps for several weeks.

Kedgeree

SERVES 6

500g smoked haddock, skinned and bones removed

360g basmati rice

1 tbsp curry powder

80g butter

480ml white chicken stock or vegetable stock (see page 122)

a pinch of pure saffron stems

4 bay leaves

2 eggs

4 spring onions

2 mild green chillies

1 bunch of coriander

salt, pepper

Preheat the oven to 200°C/gas mark 6. Melt 40g of the butter in an ovenproof pan, stir in the curry powder and cook gently for 2 or 3 minutes. Add the rice, continue to cook and stir until the rice is well coated in the butter. Pour in the stock, add the bay leaves and saffron, and bring to a simmer. Bury the haddock in the rice, keeping the fish in large pieces. Put a lid on the pan, place in the oven and bake for 15 minutes. Remove the pan from the oven, but keep the lid on for another 10 minutes.

Meanwhile, hard boil the eggs and chop them roughly. Thinly slice the spring onions and chillies, removing the chilli seeds if you don't want the dish to be too spicy.

Take the lid off the pan and fluff the rice with a fork, flaking the fish at the same time. Add the rest of the butter and check the seasoning before folding in the eggs, chillies, spring onions and chopped coriander. Serve warm.

Baguette Toast with Olive Oil, Extra-Bitter Chocolate and Sea Salt

Chocolate's feel-good factor means that many people use it as an instant lift when energy levels are low. But the immediate blood-sugar fix can become addictive and sweetened milky chocolate bars are laden with fat and empty calories. Although chocolate does have little nutritional value it is high on pleasure, so when choosing a chocolate treat have something good – you deserve it. This rather unlikely combination is absolutely delicious. Great as a snack, breakfast or pudding.

SERVES 6

18 slices of country-style thin baguette, cut at an angle into 1cm slices
480g extra-bitter chocolate, minimum 70% cocoa solids, broken into pieces
olive oil, preferably a rich peppery variety
Fleur de sel or Maldon sea salt

Preheat the oven to 130°C/gas mark 1. Lightly toast the baguette slices. Drizzle a very small amount of olive oil over each and cover with pieces of chocolate. Put the baguette slices into the oven and leave until the chocolate is just melting but not liquid. Arrange on plates, drizzle on little more olive oil and sprinkle a few salt crystals over each piece of toast.

Carpaccio of Pineapple and Coconut

SERVES 6

1 large sweet golden pineapple

fresh coconut or coconut chips (available in healthfood shops)

1 kiwi fruit

1 tbsp icing sugar

2 bunches of coriander

1 tbsp water

Peel the pineapple making sure to remove the eyes. Starting from the narrower end of the pineapple, cut into the thinnest possible slices. Take the first six slices, lay them flat on a non-stick baking mat or on greaseproof paper and cover with a sheet of greaseproof. Dry the slices in a low oven, 100°C/gas mark ½, for 3 to 4 hours or until crisp.

Take the rest of the pineapple slices, cut each slice in half and remove the core. Lay the slices on large flat plates and keep cold.

Peel the kiwi and blend it with the icing sugar, water and coriander until smooth – keep back some coriander leaves for decoration. Using a spoon, zigzag lines of the kiwi mixture on to the pineapple slices. Decorate each plate with a dried pineapple slice and scatter over some coriander leaves and coconut crisps just before serving. If using a fresh coconut, crack it open and use a peeler to make the shavings from the flesh.

'High in vitamin C, pineapple is also thought to be good for relieving bruising, sprains and blisters.'

bread

Bread is not difficult to make once you get the hang of it and home-made loaves are worth the effort. The loaves here can be made in a food processor with a dough attachment, which makes bread making even easier.
If you don't have a food processor or if you like to make bread by hand, knead for 10 minutes or so – it's a good work-out for your arms too! A few tips. I use fresh yeast but use dried if you prefer. Always sift the flour. When you put the oven on to heat up, put in a small tin with about 300ml of water. This creates some steam in the oven and stops the bread drying out as it cooks.
To check if a loaf is cooked, turn it over and tap the bottom – it should sound hollow.

Wholemeal Bread

MAKES 2 LOAVES
For the leavening:
15g fresh yeast
250ml warm water
100g strong white flour
150g wholemeal flour

For the final mix:
300g spelt flour
300g rye flour
3 tsp salt
250ml warm water

This bread is made in two stages. First, dissolve the yeast in 250ml of warm water and mix it with the strong white and wholemeal flour. Cover and leave to rise and double in volume for about 1 hour. Put this leavening mixture in the bowl of a food mixer with a dough hook. Dissolve the salt in 250ml of warm water, pour this on to the mixture and add the spelt and rye flours. Beat the dough at low speed until homogeneous or knead by hand. Cover and leave to rise and double in volume – about 2 hours.

Knock back the dough, place on a floured surface, preferably marble or wood, and shape into two large round loaves (550g) or individual rolls (40g). Put the loaves or rolls on a baking tray, cover and leave to rise for about 1 hour. Preheat the oven to 230°C/gas mark 8. Using a razor blade or a very sharp knife, score the tops to about 6mm deep and immediately place the bread in the hot oven. Bake loaves for about 1 hour or rolls for 20 minutes.

Soft Rye Bread Buns

MAKES 12–15

600g white bread flour

400g dark rye flour

40g yeast

30g milk powder

600ml lukewarm water

30g fine table salt

1 tbsp caster sugar

100g unsalted butter, melted

Dissolve the milk powder and yeast in the lukewarm water, then add the sifted flours. Put the dough in the bowl of a mixer with a dough hook and gently knead for 1 minute. Add the salt and sugar, increase the speed a little and knead for a further 5 minutes until smooth. After 3 minutes, bring down the dough from the top of the hook so that it mixes well with the rest, then pour in the lukewarm melted butter and knead until completely amalgamated. Remove the hook, cover the dough with a wet cloth and leave to rise in a warm, draught-free place for 30 minutes or until doubled in volume.

Once it has risen, knock the dough back, place it on a floured surface and shape into buns weighing 120g each. Put the buns on a baking tray, dust with a little flour, cover and leave to rise again for 20 minutes or until nearly doubled. Preheat the oven to 220°C/gas mark 7. Depending on your oven, the rolls should cook in about 16 minutes. Cool on a wire rack.

Herb and Celery Soda Bread

MAKES ONE LOAF 24 X 10CM

250g wholemeal flour

250g strong unbleached bread flour

1 tsp celery salt

1 tsp salt

1 tsp bicarbonate of soda

1 medium onion

2 sticks of celery

2 tsp celery seeds

65g butter

juice of 1 lemon

250ml milk

1 bunch of fresh mint

2 bunches of flat-leaf parsley

1 bunch of lovage (celery leaf can be used instead)

Preheat the oven to 200°C/gas mark 6. Put the flours, bicarbonate of soda and salts in a large bowl and mix together. Chop the peeled onion and the celery sticks into very small dice. Sweat in a pan with half the butter and the celery seeds until soft but not coloured. Leave to cool.

Rub the rest of the butter into the flour and add the cooled onion and celery, with all their pan juices, and mix well. Make a well in the middle of the mixture and pour in the milk and lemon juice. Mix the flour into the liquid to make a soft but not too sticky dough and add the chopped herbs. Turn the dough on to a floured surface and knead well, shaping it into an oblong loaf.

Place in a lightly greased 900g loaf tin. Using a sharp knife, cut a deep cross into the dough. Bake for 40–50 minutes or until the bread sounds hollow when tapped on the bottom. Leave to cool on a wire rack.

Irish Soda Bread

MAKES 1 LOAF

250g wholemeal flour

50g bread flour

50g oatmeal

50g wheatgerm

1½ tsp bicarbonate of soda

1½ tsp salt

1 tbsp light muscovado sugar

1 large egg

300ml buttermilk

Preheat the oven to 190°C/gas mark 5. Mix the dry ingredients together and make a well in the centre. Break the egg into the well. Using your fingertips, gradually work in some of the flour and pour in the buttermilk until all has been absorbed. The dough should be soft but not too sticky – add a little flour if it is – and don't overwork it.

Make the dough into a loaf shape, place on a baking tray. and bake for 1 hour. Cool on a wire rack.

Ceps and Garlic Confit Bread

This bread can accompany most salads, soups and meats or makes a meal on its own.

MAKES 1 LARGE LOAF
400g strong white bread flour
100g spelt flour
100g rye flour
60g dried ceps in slices
425ml warm water
25g fresh yeast
1 tbsp fresh thyme leaves picked off the stems
1 level tbsp salt
1 tbsp olive oil
12 cloves of garlic confit (see below)

Cover the ceps with 150ml of the water and leave them to soak for 30 minutes. Dissolve the yeast with the rest of the water in a mixing bowl, then stir in the white flour using a wooden spatula. Cover and leave in a warm place to rise and double in volume. Drain the ceps and pan fry in the olive oil for 1 minute. Drain again and set aside.

In the bowl of a food mixer put the soaking water of the ceps, the remaining flours, salt, thyme and the risen first dough. Knead at a low speed with the dough hook for 10 minutes. Scrape down the dough from the edges of the bowl and the hook and knead for another two minutes. Cover and leave to rise for 30 minutes.

Knock the dough back again, then gently work in the ceps and garlic without breaking them up. Do this by folding the bread over on itself several times. Shape the dough into a loaf and place on a floured baking tray. Cover and leave to rise for 30 minutes. Preheat the oven to 220°C/gas mark 7, then bake the loaf for 35–40 minutes.

Garlic Confit

Peel the garlic cloves, blanch in boiling water and drain. Put them on a piece of aluminium foil, sprinkle with a little sea salt and a generous amount of olive oil. Wrap the garlic up loosely by bringing the corners of the foil together to make a 'bag'. Put on an ovenproof dish and cook in the oven at 170°C/gas mark 3 for 1 hour. Shake the bag three or four times during the cooking. Leave to cool before using.

Rich Grain and Malt Bread

MAKES 2 LOAVES

200g strong unbleached bread flour

200g spelt flour

100g wholewheat flour

100g rye flour

20g fresh yeast

450ml water

1 level tbsp salt

3 tbsp liquid extract of malt

1 tbsp each of millet, rolled oats, linseed, sunflower seeds, bran, wheatgerm

Dissolve the yeast in half the warm water, add the flours, salt, malt and whatever seeds and grains you are using. Knead by hand or in a food mixer with a dough hook, gradually adding more water. When the dough is elastic but not sticky, stop adding water. Continue to knead for another 10 minutes. In general, the more water in the dough the lighter the bread, but this bread is better if fairly heavy. Cover and leave to rise in a warm place for 90 minutes.

Knock the dough back, turn it on to a floured surface and divide into two. Put the loaves into non-stick 450g loaf tins, cover and leave to rise again for 40 minutes. Cook in a pre-heated oven at 230°C/gas mark 8 for 10 minutes then turn the oven down to 200°C/gas mark 6 for a further 30 minutes or until cooked. Cool on a wire rack.

Hamstring stretch

The 'marathon' is named after a plain in ancient Greece. In 490BC a runner named Pheidippides sped about 240 kilometres from Marathon to Athens with the news that the Greeks had won a great victory over the Persians in the Persian Wars.

Cheese and Marjoram Rolls

MAKES 30 ROLLS

1kg strong, unbleached, stoneground bread flour

25g fresh yeast

460ml warm water

100ml warm milk, plus some extra for brushing the rolls

2 tsp salt

20g caster sugar

1 egg

2 tbsp olive oil

100g Parmesan cheese, freshly grated

1 bunch of marjoram. leaves picked from the stems

300g Cheddar or Emmenthal cheese, cut into 30 thin slices

Dissolve the yeast in the warm water and milk, and add the flour, salt, sugar, egg and oil. Knead by hand or in a food mixer with a dough hook for 12–15 minutes. Cover and leave to rise for 90 minutes.

Knock back the dough and mix in the Parmesan cheese and marjoram leaves without overworking. Divide into 30 pieces, each weighing about 60g, and place on a non-stick baking tray. Cover and leave to rise for 20 minutes.

Preheat the oven to 190°C/gas mark 5. Brush the rolls with a little milk. Using a pair of sharp scissors, cut a deep cross on the top of each roll and insert a thin slice of mature Cheddar or Emmenthal cheese. Bake the rolls for 25 to 30 minutes and cool on a wire rack.

Black Pepper Baps

12–14 ROLLS

500g strong bread flour

20g fresh yeast

300ml warm milk

1 tbsp caster sugar

2 tsp salt

20g cracked black peppercorns

Dissolve the yeast in the milk and gradually add the flour, sugar, salt and peppercorns. Knead the dough in a food mixer or by hand until it is elastic yet supple. Cover and leave in a warm place to double in volume, about 30 minutes.

Knock the dough back and place on a floured surface. Divide it into 12–14 balls of about 60g, cup your hand over each ball and 'turn' them until smooth and perfectly round. Put these on a floured baking tray, cover with a cloth and leave to rise for 20 minutes. Preheat the oven to 220°C/gas mark 7. Bake the rolls for 15–20 minutes.

Fruit and Nut Bread

MAKES 3 LOAVES

1.2kg strong white bread flour

1.25 litres warm water

50g fresh yeast

35g salt

125g light rye flour

375g wholemeal flour

100g sultanas

100g walnuts

60g hazelnuts

60g dried apricots, sliced

Melt the yeast in a litre of water and add the white flour and salt. Knead the dough in a food mixer with the dough hook attachment or by hand until it is elastic and comes away from the sides of the bowl – about 10 minutes. Cover with a damp cloth and leave in a warm, draught-free place to rise and double in volume – 60–90 minutes.

Knead again, by machine or hand, and add the remaining 250ml of water with the rye and wholemeal flours. Continue kneading until the flours are completely amalgamated then gently mix in the fruit and nuts by hand. Shape into three long loaves and place on a non-stick baking sheet or put into lightly greased bread tins. Cover the loaves with a damp cloth and leave to rise by a third, which should take about 30 minutes. Preheat the oven to 250°C/gas mark 9.

Put the loaves into the hot oven and turn down the temperature to 220°C/gas mark 7. The cooking time depends on your oven but they should take 25–35 minutes. Check that a loaf sounds hollow when tapped underneath. Leave to cool on a wire rack. Great toasted for breakfast or with cheese.

Italian Ciabatta

MAKES 1 LOAF

265g strong white bread flour

12g fresh yeast

200ml warm water

1 tsp salt

3 tbsp olive oil

Dissolve the yeast in the warm water and add the sifted flour and salt. The mixture will feel wet and sticky at first but don't add any more flour. Work the dough for 5 or 6 minutes until smooth. Lightly grease a bowl with a little of the olive oil and put in the dough. Cover with clingfilm and leave in a warm place for 40 minutes.

Knock back the dough and add the rest of the olive oil, but don't over-work. Put the dough on a floured baking tray and shape into a loaf about 28cm long. Flatten it lightly and flour the top. Cover with a dry cloth and leave to rise again for 40 minutes. Preheat the oven to 220°C/gas mark 7 and bake the loaf for 30 to 35 minutes. Cool on a wire rack.

Fougasse Bread with Olives

MAKES 1 LARGE LOAF

500g strong unbleached bread flour

1 heaped tsp salt

20g fresh yeast

300ml lukewarm water

4 tbsp olive oil

1 tbsp of thyme and rosemary leaves, picked from their stems

85g mixed pitted olives, best quality, not the ones in brine that have little or no taste

Sift the flour with the salt, dissolve the yeast in the lukewarm water and mix together to make the dough. Knead for at least 12 minutes, cover and leave to rise for 45 minutes.

Turn on to a floured surface and mix in the olives, olive oil and thyme and rosemary leaves. Make the dough into a ball, then roll it out to 15mm thick. Transfer this to a non-stick baking tray, then cut through the dough six times to make a leaf pattern, pulling on the dough to make the holes bigger. Cover and leave to rise again for 20–30 minutes. Preheat the oven to 230°C/gas mark 8 and bake the loaf for 20 minutes.

Focaccia with Basil, Garlic and Anchovies

MAKES 1 LARGE LOAF
750g strong bread flour
350ml lukewarm water
25g fresh yeast
3 tbsp olive oil
1 heaped tsp sugar
2 tsp salt
1 bunch of basil
2 cloves of garlic
12 anchovy fillets
black pepper

Dissolve the yeast in the lukewarm water, add to the sifted flour and knead in the olive oil, sugar and salt. When the dough is smooth and elastic, cover the bowl and leave to rise and double in size – 30–40 minutes.

Roll out the dough on a lightly floured surface to a thickness of 2cm. Place on a non-stick baking sheet, make several cuts in the centre of the bread and pull the dough from the edges. Cover the surface evenly with anchovies, basil leaves and coarsely chopped garlic, sprinkle with a little crushed black pepper and leave to rise again for 20 minutes. Preheat the oven to 220°C/gas mark 7 and bake the loaf for 20–30 minutes.

Olive Oil Bread

MAKES 1 LOAF
500g strong, unbleached, stoneground bread flour
12g fresh yeast
275ml warm water
4 tbsp olive oil
1 heaped tsp fine salt and a pinch of coarse sea salt

Dissolve the yeast in the warm water, add the flour and knead for 15 minutes until silken and elastic. Add the olive oil and fine salt and knead again for 5 minutes. Cover and leave to rise for 40 minutes. Knock back the dough and form it into a long loaf. Place on a non-stick baking sheet, cover and leave to rise for another 20 minutes. Preheat the oven to 230°C/gas mark 8. Lightly brush the top of the loaf with milk, add a sprinkling of coarse sea salt, then bake for 30 minutes or until cooked.

Goat's Cheese Bread

MAKES 12 ROLLS OR 1 BIG LOAF

600g spelt flour (or unbleached white bread flour)

60g boiled potato

1 heaped tsp fine table salt

15g fresh yeast

250ml warm water

2 tbsp olive oil

65g dry goat's cheese (crottin or similar)

1 tbsp of thyme and rosemary leaves, picked from their stems

coarse sea salt

Dissolve the yeast in the warm water and add the flour, crushed potato and fine salt. Knead in a food mixer with a dough hook or by hand for 10 minutes until elastic and smooth. Cover and leave in a warm place to rise until double the volume – about 45 minute.

Knock back the dough and divide into 12 rolls or roll out to make one loaf about 2cm thick. Place on a lightly oiled baking sheet. Crumble the cheese and push it on to the surface of the bread. Sprinkle with thyme, rosemary and a little coarse sea salt, drizzle with olive oil and leave to rise for another 15 minutes. Preheat the oven to 220°C/gas mark 7. Bake rolls for 20 minutes or a loaf for 30–40 minutes.

A marathon race was included in the first modern Olympic Games held in Athens in 1896. The course was 40 kilometres long and the race was won by Greek runner Spiridon Louis in two hours, 58 minutes and 50 seconds.

Corn and Fennel Seed Bread

MAKES 1 LARGE LOAF

200g strong white flour
250g fine polenta
30g fresh yeast
2 tbsp honey
150ml warm water
250ml milk and 1 tbsp for brushing the loaf
1 tsp salt
2 tbsp fennel seeds

Dissolve the yeast in the warm water and honey. Add half the sifted flour to make a very wet paste. Cover and leave in a warm place to rest for 30 minutes.

Put the rest of the ingredients in the bowl of a food mixer with a dough hook attachment – keep back one tablespoon of fennel seeds to decorate the loaf. Pour in the first mix after it has rested and work to a smooth elastic dough.

Put the dough in a large 24 x 8cm loaf tin or divide it into mini-loaf tins, 3 x 5cm. Cover and leave in a warm place to rise for 30 minutes. Preheat the oven to 220°C/gas mark 7. Before putting the bread in the oven, brush the top with a little milk and sprinkle with the remaining seeds. Bake for 20–30 minutes depending on size.

Thigh stretch

soups and starters

Lentil Soup with Thyme

SERVES 6

400g green Puy lentils

1 stick of celery

1 small carrot

1 onion

1 garlic clove

4 slices of smoked streaky bacon

1 tbsp olive oil

1 litre white chicken stock (see page 122)

salt, pepper

1 bunch of thyme

Peel the vegetables and cut into small dice. Cut the bacon into matchstick strips. Heat the olive oil in a heavy-based saucepan and add the bacon and vegetables. Cook, stirring occasionally, until golden.

Rinse the lentils under cold water and add to the vegetables. Pour on the stock, quickly bring to the boil, then reduce the heat and simmer for about 45 minutes until the lentils are tender. Check the seasoning and sprinkle with thyme leaves. Serve with black pepper baps (page 54) or corn and fennel seed bread (page 61).

If you prefer to serve this soup smooth, blend it briefly, saving a few spoonfuls of the lentils to garnish.

Drink plenty of water

The current marathon distance is 26 miles and 385 yards (42.16km). This was set at the London Olympics of 1908 so that the race could begin at Windsor Castle and finish in front of the royal box at White City Stadium, and it is now the standard.

Garlic and Sage Soup

A traditional soup from the South of France, this is called *l'aigo boulido* –
literally 'boiled garlic'. Garlic is antibacterial, antiviral and a decongestant,
and this soup is often prescribed for people who are feeling under the weather
or in need of some detox! It is enhanced by a touch of sage, which is also a
mild antiseptic and aids digestion. Every household in le Midi has its own
method and recipe of *l'aigo boulido*, but everyone agrees it's best to use new-
season garlic when it is sweet and innocuous. Wild garlic, which grows in
abundance beside streams in Britain in the early summer, can also be used.
If using wild garlic, allow 1 leaf per clove, but do not cook the leaves – just
roughly chop and add at the last second. Alternatively use a mixture of cloves
and leaves.

SERVES 4

20 or more cloves of garlic to taste

1 litre water

coarse sea salt

8 sage leaves

2 tbsp strong thick olive oil

12 thick slices of stale country-style bread

Peel the garlic and slice each clove into 5 or 6 slices. Put the garlic into a
saucepan with the water and salt, bring to the boil and simmer for 30
minutes. Add the sliced sage leaves and take off the heat. Serve piping hot.

Tradition has it that you put the stale bread in the bottom of the bowl and
pour over the soup, with or without a drizzle of olive oil. When you've eaten
all but a few spoonfuls of soup, pour a dose of wine into your bowl before
finishing it off – purely medicinal of course!

Squash and Shrimp Soup with Nutmeg

If using small squash the soup can be served in the hollowed-out skins or a big pumpkin can brought to the table as a tureen.

SERVES 4

4 x 175g squash or 1 x 700g pumpkin, unpeeled weight
4 shallots
olive oil
1 litre white chicken stock or vegetable stock (see page 122)
200g peeled brown shrimps
salt, pepper, nutmeg

If using the squash or pumpkin for serving this soup, slice off the top and hollow out the flesh and seeds using a spoon. Otherwise, cut away the skin with a knife. Cut the flesh into very small dice and peel and chop the shallots. Sweat the vegetables in a little olive oil until soft but not coloured. Season with a generous amount of salt, pepper and nutmeg, then pour in the chicken stock. Bring to a simmer and cook for 20 minutes, then blend until smooth. Add the shrimps just before serving. Accompany with pumpkin seed biscuits.

Pumpkin Seed Biscuits

200g plain flour
1 tsp baking powder
a pinch of salt and a pinch of cayenne pepper
100g medium oatmeal
60g unsalted butter, softened
80g mature cheddar, grated
1 egg
120g pumpkin seeds
milk

Sift the flour with the salt, cayenne and baking powder and add the oatmeal. Rub in the soft butter to make a fine sandy texture, then add the cheese, egg and 80g of pumpkin seeds with a little milk if needed. Don't overwork the dough, but bring it together, wrap in film and refrigerate for 20 minutes. Preheat the oven to 180°C/gas mark 4. Roll the dough out to a thickness of 3–5mm and cut to the size you want. Brush with milk and sprinkle with the remaining pumpkin seeds. Place on a non-stick baking tray and bake for 15–20 minutes. Cool slightly before removing the biscuits from the tray.

Chestnut and Apple Soup with Rosemary

Unlike most other nuts, chestnuts are high in complex carbohydrates in the form of fibre and starch. They are also virtually fat free. I was once ushered away at gunpoint from an area in the Cévennes region of France where the sweetest chestnuts are grown and gathered. The early-season crop is highly prized and the locals protect their trees with vigour!

SERVES 6

1kg fresh chestnuts

1 litre water

2 tbsp maple syrup

2 sprigs of rosemary

4 apples, Coxes or similar

salt, pepper

Score the chestnuts with a sharp-pointed knife to prevent them exploding in the oven while roasting. Lay them out on a roasting tray and cook in a hot oven, 230°C/gas mark 8, for 12–15 minutes. When cool enough to handle, remove the outer shells and then the skin.

Keep 12 perfectly shaped chestnuts for the garnish and put the rest in a pan with the water. Bring to the boil, season, then add the maple syrup and sprigs of rosemary and simmer for 20 minutes. Remove the rosemary, blend the soup until smooth and return to a saucepan. Peel, core and finely dice the apple and add to the boiling soup. Leave to cook for 3 minutes before pouring into hot bowls and garnishing with the whole peeled chestnuts.

Watercress Soup

SERVES 4

600g watercress
180g potatoes
600ml boiling salted water
white pepper, ground
salt
crème fraîche (optional)

Chop off the lower part of the watercress stems. Wash the watercress in
several changes of water and remove any yellow leaves. Peel the potatoes and
cut into small dice, 5 x 5mm. Cook 80g of the diced potatoes in boiling water
to use as a garnish and set aside.

Heat a large pan until scalding hot, add the watercress and stir as it wilts.
Pour in the 600ml of water and add the remaining uncooked diced potatoes.
Season with salt and white pepper and simmer until the diced potato is
cooked, 8–10 minutes. Blend or process the soup until smooth and press it
through a fine conical strainer. Do this whole operation as quickly as you can
to keep the soup's vivid green colour. Serve hot or cold in individual bowls
with the diced potato garnish. A spoonful of crème fraîche added just before
serving is delicious and not too decadent.

Cock-a-Leekie Soup

SERVES 6

1.5 litres white chicken stock (see page 122)
200g leeks, white and yellow leaves only
100g prunes, stoned
100g cooked chicken
parsley, chopped
salt, pepper

This is a good way to use up any left-over roast chicken. Use the carcass for
the stock.

Bring the stock to the boil and season. Clean and shred the leeks, add them
to the stock and simmer for 15–20 minutes. Cut the chicken and prunes into
fine strips, add both to the soup and simmer for another 2 minutes. Check the
seasoning, sprinkle with chopped parsley and serve piping hot.

Cockle, Clam and Shrimp Broth with Angel-Hair Pasta

Angel-hair pasta can be found in most good delicatessens but you can also use Chinese glass noodles.

SERVES 6

1kg live cockles in their shells

1kg Venus clams or surf clams in their shells

120g angel-hair pasta

75cl dry white wine such as Chardonnay

300ml water

200g peeled brown shrimps

3 spring onions

1 red chilli, finely sliced

1 bunch of flat-leaf parsley

olive oil

Make sure the cockles and clams are very fresh and not gaping. Soak them in cold water for 20 minutes to clean them and remove any sand.

Heat a large saucepan over high heat. Add the drained shellfish, wine and water and cover with a lid. Leave over a high heat, giving the pan a shake now and then to make sure the shellfish are cooking evenly. Cooking time depends on how hot your stove is, but when the shells have opened and you can easily remove the flesh the shellfish are cooked. This usually takes 4–6 minutes. Place a colander over a bowl big enough to collect the cooking liquor and empty the shellfish into it. Pick all the meat out of the shells and put aside. Pass the liquor through a muslin cloth to remove any sand.

Divide the cockles, clams and shrimp equally between six soup plates and add some thinly sliced spring onions and chilli to each one. Bring the liquor back to the boil, check the seasoning and cook the pasta in this for a matter of seconds. Pour some scalding hot liquid and pasta into each bowl, add a drizzle of olive oil and some coarsely chopped parsley and serve immediately.

Leek and Lobster Salad with Mango Vinaigrette

SERVES 4

4 large leeks

2 lobsters, each weighing about 500g

juice of 1 lemon

1 bunch of basil

1 very ripe mango

2 tbsp olive oil

2 tbsp water

salt, pepper

Trim the leeks and rinse under cold water. Cut off the dark green leaves at the top and discard. Starting at the top, slice the leeks diagonally until you have 6cm left of the white. Leave this part whole. Cook the sliced leek and the white stems separately in lots of boiling salted water until tender, refresh in iced water and drain.

Cook the lobsters in boiling salted water for 8 minutes. When they are cool enough to handle, break them open, remove the flesh and cut into médaillons.

Season the sliced leeks with a little salt, pepper, 1 tablespoon of olive oil and half the lemon juice. Cut the white stems in half lengthways. To serve, place some sliced leeks on each plate and a halved leek stem on top. Tuck some pieces of lobster in between the leek stems and arrange the claws at the sides. Drizzle with the mango vinaigrette and decorate with a few pieces of diced mango and basil leaves. This dish is best served at room temperature so do not prepare it too far in advance.

Mango Vinaigrette

Blend half the peeled mango, a little salt, pepper, most of the basil (keeping some leaves for decoration), half the lemon juice, 1 tablespoon of olive oil and 2 tablespoon of water together until smooth.

Pea and Broad Bean Salad with Fresh Mint and Scallops

SERVES 4

200g fresh peas, shelled

200g fresh broad beans, shelled

12 scallops with their coral

1 bunch of mint

2 spring onions, sliced

4 tbsp olive oil

2 tbsp sweet, well-aged balsamic vinegar

pepper, coarse sea salt

Blanch the peas and broad beans in boiling salted water, then plunge them into iced water to retain their vibrant green colour and halt the cooking. Keep them slightly underdone. Drain and remove the skins of the broad beans, which tend to be hard and bitter. Large peas could also be skinned. Coarsely chop the mint leaves and mix with the peas, beans, sliced spring onions and olive oil. Arrange the salad on four plates and season with sea salt and pepper.

Smear a non-stick frying pan with olive oil and cook the scallops over high heat until caramelized on both sides. They should take about 30 seconds each side, depending on their size. Season and arrange neatly on the salad. Drizzle over some balsamic vinegar and serve immediately.

Oysters with Red Wine Shallot Vinegar

My preference is for 'native' oysters – the flat variety. They are slightly more expensive and harder to open than other types but are truly delicious. The 'Pacific' or 'Rock' variety are also good, but if you are going to eat oysters raw in the half shell, go for the best. Oysters are easily digested and rich in zinc. They are great for fighting the common cold and good for your libido!

This red wine shallot vinegar is traditionally served with oysters, but other accompaniments such as lemon, Tabasco and freshly ground pepper are also good. Six oysters per person is the usual serving but allow 12 if feeling greedy.

SERVES 4

6 oysters per person

2 medium shallots finely chopped

100ml red wine vinegar

Add the shallots to the vinegar and leave to steep for at least an hour. Open the oysters at the last possible moment. Always buy from a reputable fishmonger and make sure the oysters are still alive and tightly closed. They should feel heavy when you pick them up and sound full when tapped together. Serve with toasted wholemeal bread and the shallot vinegar.

Calf stretch

Khalid Khannouchi of the USA set the record for the fastest marathon by a male runner at the 2002 London Marathon with a time of two hours, five minutes and 38 seconds.

Oysters with Horseradish and Tuna Tartare

SERVES 6

36 medium native oysters

360g fresh tuna loin

1 tbsp horseradish relish

3 spring onions, thinly sliced

1 bunch of watercress

1 celery heart

3 plum tomatoes

salt, pepper, Worcestershire sauce

Cut the tuna into small dice and put in a bowl set over ice. Fold in the horseradish and spring onions and salt and pepper to taste. Do not do this more than 30 minutes before serving otherwise the acidity in the relish will 'burn' the tuna.

Open the oysters and remove the flesh, taking care to take out any pieces of shell that may have chipped into the oyster. Keep any juice from the shells. Put a spoonful of tuna into each shell and add an oyster on top. Decorate with a few watercress and celery leaves and pour on a little tomato sauce. Arrange the oysters on a bed of crushed ice or on special oyster plates.

Tomato Sauce

Blanch the tomatoes in boiling water for 12 seconds and refresh in iced water. Peel and remove the seeds. Take the juice collected from the oysters and pass it through a fine sieve. Blend the tomato flesh and sieved oyster juices until smooth and season with Worcestershire sauce.

Raw Marinated Scallops with Orange and Honey Dressing

SERVES 6

18 extra-large scallops (more if small)

juice of ½ a lemon

juice of 2 oranges

2 tbsp orange-flower honey

120ml light olive oil

salt, pepper

Make sure the scallops are the freshest possible and not soaked. Ideally, buy them in the shell – this means a little extra work but is a sure way of knowing they are alive. Having shelled the scallops if necessary, rinse them under cold water and pat dry with kitchen towel.

To make the vinaigrette, blend the lemon and orange juice with the honey and a pinch of salt. Gradually add the olive oil – the vinaigrette should emulsify and look rich and frothy.

Cut the scallops across into slices 3mm thick. Lay the slices on a large plate or dish, drizzle a little vinaigrette over them and refrigerate for an hour before serving.

The salad

2 bunches of watercress

2 oranges

3 small red Belgian endives

1 small bunch of chives

pepper, salt

Pick the watercress into small florets and wash gently in cold water. Dry in a salad spinner and put aside. Peel the oranges, making sure to remove the pith. Cut into segments, removing the membrane. Cut the endive into individual leaves and the chives into batons 4cm long. Toss the watercress and endive in a little of the vinaigrette and add salt if needed.

To serve

Arrange the scallops on individual plates in a circle, add some orange segments and a little salad in the centre. Drizzle some more vinaigrette around the plates, sprinkle with chives and finish with a generous amount of coarsely ground pepper.

Fillet of John Dory with Coconut and Lime Salad

SERVES 6

1 John Dory weighing about 900g

1 coconut

1 tbsp caster sugar

1 bulb of fennel

2 limes

2 spring onions

2 bunches of opal basil

30ml light olive oil

salt, pepper

Fillet the John Dory, remove the skin – the fishmonger should do this if you ask. Divide each fillet into nine portions. Crack the coconut with a mallet or the back of a cleaver, taking care to collect the juice. Finely grate half the coconut flesh into the juice and add the caster sugar. Cover and refrigerate for 1 hour, then press through a muslin cloth to get a fine coconut cream. If there is no juice or very little in the coconut add a little water.

Using a Japanese vegetable slicer, cut the rest of the coconut and the fennel into very thin slices. Peel the limes with a paring knife and split them into segments. Thinly slice the spring onions. Lightly toss the fennel, coconut, spring onion and most of the basil (save some for decoration) with the lime segments, olive oil, salt and pepper.

In a scalding hot non-stick pan smeared with olive oil, sear the seasoned John Dory on both sides until golden but still 'pink' inside.

To assemble the dish, pour some coconut cream on to each plate, add some fennel salad and three pieces of fish. Top with a little more salad and a basil leaf or two.

Tartare of Mackerel with Pink Pepper

Since this dish is eaten raw, it's even more important than usual that the mackerel is extremely fresh. The fish should be glistening, shiny and firm.

SERVES 4

2 very fresh mackerel

1 bunch of radishes

1 bunch of watercress

1 bulb of fennel

juice of 1 large lemon

3 spring onions

1 bunch of dill or fennel weed

2 tbsp olive oil

salt

1 tsp dry pink peppercorns

Fillet and skin the mackerel. Remove the tiny bones in the middle of the fillet and cut into 4mm dice. Put the diced fish in a bowl set over ice to keep it very cold. The seasoning of the tartare must be done at the very last moment otherwise it will 'burn' – the texture of the fish will change from soft to rubbery and it will leech all its natural juices.

Wash and thinly slice the radishes. Wash and dry the watercress and pick into little florets. Using a vegetable slicer, cut the fennel into paper-thin slices and season them with a little lemon juice, salt, pepper and olive oil.

Arrange a circle of fennel slices in the centre of each plate. Put some radish slices around them and season with a vinaigrette made with 1 tablespoon of olive oil, 1 teaspoon of lemon juice, 1 tablespoon of water, salt and pepper.

Finally, season the mackerel by gently folding in lemon juice to taste, salt, pink pepper, spring onions and chopped dill or fennel weed. Using a metal ring or a pastry cutter, mould a ring of fish on top of the fennel salad on each plate. Decorate with some watercress.

Linguine and Shrimp Salad with Basil and Dried Tomatoes

SERVES 6

360g egg linguine

6 large plum tomatoes

200g peeled brown shrimps

1 bunch of basil

2 spring onions

1 clove of garlic

zest of 1 lemon, grated

4 tbsp strong dark olive oil

4 tbsp balsamic vinegar

salt, pepper

Blanch the tomatoes in boiling water and refresh. Peel, cut in half and remove the seeds. Brush the tomato halves with olive oil and place them on a wire rack. Bake in the oven at 100°C/gas mark ½ for 75 minutes or until dry but not coloured.

Cook the linguine in plenty of boiling salted water until al dente. Drain, refresh under cold water and mix in a tablespoon of olive oil to prevent sticking. Finely slice the basil, leaving a few leaves for decoration. Finely slice the spring onions and chop the garlic. Mix the basil, onions and garlic into the linguine with the shrimps, the rest of the olive oil, grated lemon zest, salt and pepper. Using a kitchen fork, twirl the pasta into 6 nests and place on cold plates with some dried tomatoes on each side. Decorate with a basil leaf and drizzle with balsamic vinegar.

Back and hamstring stretch

The current record for a female runner was set by Catherine N'dereba from Kenya with a time of two hours, 18 minutes and 47 seconds at the Chicago Marathon in October 2001.

Cheddar Cheese and Prune Relish 'Mille-Feuille'

SERVES 6

12 slices of cheddar, about 8 x 4cm and 3mm thick

3 little gem lettuces

2 large ripe beef tomatoes

1 bunch of basil

3 tbsp olive oil

1 tsp red wine vinegar

2 tbsp water

1 clove of garlic

salt, pepper

To make the vinaigrette, blend the basil (keeping some leaves for decoration) with the olive oil, vinegar, water, garlic and a little seasoning until smooth. This can also be done in a mortar.

Cut the little gems lengthways into 4 even slices. Cut the tomatoes across into 4 slices. Build a 'mille-feuille' on each plate by layering slices of tomato, lettuce and cheese. Season lightly. Finish with a spoonful of prune relish and some basil, then drizzle vinaigrette around the 'mille-feuille'.

Prune Relish

300g pitted prunes

500g tomatoes

1kg Bramley apples

350g onions

600ml cider vinegar

600g light muscovado sugar

½ tbsp English mustard powder

1 tsp ground cinnamon

1 heaped tsp salt

pinch of cayenne pepper or chilli powder

Blanch and skin the tomatoes. Cut in half, scoop out the seeds, chop them roughly and leave to drain. Peel and grate the apples. Peel and slice the onions.

Put the apples, onions, vinegar, sugar, mustard, salt, cinnamon and cayenne or chilli into a heavy-based pan. Cook over medium heat for about 30 minutes, stirring occasionally, until the mixture has thickened and the moisture left is syrupy. Add the chopped tomatoes and halved prunes and continue to cook at a gentle simmer for another 30 minutes, adding a little water if the mixture gets too dry. Pour into clean glass jars and refrigerate.

This relish keeps for several months and is delicious served with hard cheese or cold meats.

Grilled Tiger Prawns with Cucumber Salad and Pistachio Yogurt Dressing

SERVES 4

12 medium-sized tiger prawns

1 large cucumber

120g peeled pistachios

150g plain Greek-style yogurt

olive oil

salt, pepper

Peel the tiger prawns, leaving the tip of the tail intact. Using a sharp knife, cut down the back to remove the intestine. Peel the cucumber, cut it in half lengthways and remove the seeds. Cut in half again to give four pieces, about 14cm long. Using a Japanese vegetable slicer, cut the cucumber into fine, long julienne strips, season with salt and place in a colander to drain. After about 30 minutes the salt will have leeched the water out of the cucumber. Lightly squeeze the cucumber strips, place them in a bowl and fold in half the yogurt. Season with a generous amount of pepper.

Put the rest of the yogurt in a blender with half the pistachios. Season with salt and pepper, then blitz to a fine purée – you can also do this in a mortar. Finely chop the rest of the pistachios.

Smear a little olive oil on a very hot non-stick pan. Place the prawns in the pan and cook over high heat for 2 minutes each side. Season with salt and pepper. Using a kitchen fork, make twirls of cucumber, as you would pasta, and place one in the centre of each plate. Arrange three tiger prawns around the cucumber, drizzle on some yogurt sauce and sprinkle with chopped pistachios.

Smoked Eel, Potato Cake and Tomato Chutney

1 smoked eel, about 1.2kg, or 800g of smoked eel fillet

2 large potatoes, Desirée or King Edward

4 spring onions

olive oil, salt, pepper

If using a whole smoked eel, fillet by following the backbone with a sharp knife from the head to the tail and then pulling the skin off. If you have fillets, cut them into large diamonds 3cm wide. Grate or 'julienne' the peeled potato into a cloth and press to dry. Do not wash the potato or you will wash away the starch that holds the cake together.

Heat 6 little non-stick pans and smear them with olive oil or put metal crumpet rings into a lightly oiled frying pan. Season the potato and mix in 2 sliced spring onions. Press this mixture into the pans or rings and cook over medium heat, pressing the potato down several times to set it. After 5–6 minutes it should be golden and crisp. Turn over to cook on other side, pressing again to shape and set. Depending on the thickness of the potato cakes you may need to finish cooking them in the oven for 10 minutes at 200°C/gas mark 6.

Cut the remaining spring onions into very fine julienne strips and put in iced water to curl. Serve the potato cakes warm with slices of smoked eel stacked on top and some julienne of spring onion to decorate. Add some tomato chutney at the side.

Spicy Tomato Chutney
MAKES 2 JARS

600g bright red tomatoes

½ tsp powdered ginger

1 tsp chilli powder

2 tsp salt

2 tsp tomato paste

3 cloves of garlic

125ml malt vinegar

120g light muscovado sugar

50g raisins

Blanch and skin the tomatoes. Cut them in half, remove the seeds and chop them roughly. Put the chopped tomatoes in a pan with the ginger, chilli, salt, tomato paste and finely chopped garlic. Simmer over a low heat until pulpy. Add the vinegar, sugar and raisins and simmer, stirring occasionally to prevent sticking, until the mixture thickens. Put into clean, dry jars and store in the refrigerator.

Smoked Haddock and Potato Terrine

SERVES 10–12

2 x 300–400g fillets undyed smoked haddock

milk

6 medium potatoes such as Maris Piper

4 tbsp olive oil

2 tbsp red wine vinegar

1 tbsp coarse grain mustard

2 red onions, finely chopped

500g baby spinach leaves

salt, pepper

Take a terrine measuring approximately 24 x 8 x 7cm and double line it with clingfilm, overlapping the edges by at least 8cm.

Place the haddock fillets in a pan or baking tray large enough for them to lie flat and cover with a mixture of half milk, half water. Set the pan over a high heat and as soon as the liquid trembles and is too hot to put your fingers into, stop the cooking. Remove from the heat and leave to cool. The haddock will be cooked, but moist and delicate in texture. Remove the bones and skin, keeping the pieces of fish as large as you can.

Boil the potatoes in their skins in salted water. When they are cool enough to handle, skin and cut into slices 1cm thick. Make a vinaigrette with the oil, mustard, vinegar, salt and pepper and pour some over the potatoes while they are still warm.

Fill the terrine with layers of potatoes and fish. Start with the potatoes, squaring them off to make them fit snugly, followed by a layer of fish generously sprinkled with finely chopped red onion. Repeat the layers until the terrine is full. Fold over the clingfilm and weight the terrine down, either by putting another terrine of the same size on top or a piece of wood and some weights. Refrigerate for at least 6 hours or, better still, overnight.

Serve with a salad made with the baby spinach leaves, dressed in the leftover vinaigrette. If you're feeling extravagant, add a generous spoonful of caviar to each serving.

main courses

Saturated and unsaturated fats The debate on fats can be a minefield, but put simply saturated fats are 'naughty but nice', and unsaturated fats are just 'nice'. Foods such as dairy products and red meats are classified as saturated, but they are delicious – and good for you if unadulterated and eaten in moderation. In my view there is nothing wrong with eating a bowl of raspberries with a big dollop of crème fraîche as long as you don't overdo it and eat sensibly most of the time.

The greatest danger lies in processed foods and fast or convenience foods. I avoid them at all costs. One of my pet hates is the hydrogenated vegetable oil/fat found in many pre-cooked meals, cakes or spreads. It tastes awful and you would be better off using lard – at least it's natural.

Unsaturated fats, such as olive oil, corn oil and the oils found in fish, are good for you, although too much of any fat can have health risks. As a runner I tend to cut back on fats, but as long as you are running regularly there can be no harm in the occasional full-fat yogurt or helping of real butter on hot toast. In fact, marathon and distance runners use fat reserves in the body as fuel when glycogen levels are depleted, so there's a good excuse for your buttered toast if you need one.

Grilled Turbot T-Bone Steak with Beetroot Vinaigrette, Button Mushrooms and Courgettes

To cut T-bone steaks from a turbot you need a fish of at least 5kg. Remove the head and fins, then cut it in half along the back bone. Once the fish is cut in half, slice across to make steaks of about 2cm thick. This is tricky, so if you're a novice it's best to let your fishmonger do the work for you.

SERVES 6

6 T-bone steaks of turbot, each about 220g and 2cm thick

olive oil

360g button mushrooms

2 courgettes

juice of 1 lemon

1 bunch of basil

salt, pepper

Preheat the oven to 200°C/gas mark 6. Brush the turbot steaks lightly with olive oil and season. Cook on a stovetop cast-iron griddle for 2 minutes, then give the fish a half turn to get a nice grilled patchwork effect. Repeat and then flip over and grill the other side. Place the steaks in the preheated oven to finish cooking – they could take up to 8 minutes in total. Once cooked the outer skin is easily removed.

Remove the stalks of the mushrooms and wash them if sandy. Top and tail the courgettes and cut into batons 4 x 0.5cm. In a non-stick pan smeared with a little olive oil, sear the courgettes over a high heat until they are golden brown but still firm. Remove them from the pan and add the mushrooms and lemon juice. Turn the heat down to a simmer, season and partially cover. After 4 minutes return the courgettes to the pan, add the basil and cook for a further 30 seconds. To serve, put some vegetables on each plate, top with the fish and drizzle on some beetroot vinaigrette.

Beetroot Vinaigrette

120g cooked beetroot (preferably baked as they will be sweeter)

100ml white chicken stock or vegetable stock (see page 122)

1 tbsp olive oil and 2 tsp red wine vinegar

salt, pepper

Peel the beetroot and put it in a liquidizer or food processor with the rest of the ingredients. Blend until smooth and emulsified.

Roast Gilt-head Bream with Mustard and Parsley

SERVES 4

2 x 500g gilt-head bream

8 plum tomatoes

2 shallots

4 tbsp olive oil

100ml dry white wine

60ml water

1 tbsp Pommerey grain mustard

1 bunch of flat-leaf parsley

salt, pepper

Fillet and remove the tiny pin bones from the fish with a pair of tweezers. Blanch, refresh and skin the tomatoes, then de-seed them and cut into large dice. Peel and chop the shallots and wash and roughly chop the parsley.

Smear a large non-stick frying pan with a little olive oil. Season the fish and cook over a high heat, skin-side down, until golden. Turn the fish over and continue to cook for 20 seconds. Remove from the pan and keep warm.

Add the shallots to the pan and cook over a high heat for 30 seconds, stirring all the time with a wooden spoon, so they are lightly caramelized. Add the wine and water and reduce by half. Whisk in the tomatoes, mustard, remaining olive oil and finally the parsley.

To serve, cook 80g of tagliatelle per person. On each plate, rest a fillet of fish on a bed of pasta and add the mustard and parsley sauce.

*'Fish and vegetables –
an ideal meal the night
before a marathon.'*

Tuna Belly with Spicy Mango Salsa

SERVES 6

720g skinned tuna belly, cut into 6 x 120g pieces

2 large underripe mangoes

1 ripe papaya

juice of 2 limes

juice of 1 orange

1 red and 1 green chilli

2 red onions

1 bunch of coriander and ½ a bunch of mint

olive oil

salt

Peel the mangos and papaya, cut into small dice and add the orange and lime juice. Chop the chillies, peel and chop the red onion and add these to the fruit. Season. Just before serving, fold in the roughly chopped herbs.

Sear the tuna over a high heat in a non-stick pan with a drop of olive oil – the tuna is best kept very pink. Drain 1 tablespoon of juice from the salsa, add 2 tablespoons of olive oil and use this to season an accompanying salad of purslane or mâche (lamb's lettuce). Serve the tuna on a bed of salsa.

Stuffed Sea Bass with Creole Rice

SERVES 2

1.2kg sea bass (preferably wild not farmed)

60g long-grain rice

1 red pepper

4 shallots

2 cloves of garlic

3 curry leaves

1 mild red and 1 green chilli

1 large bunch of fresh coriander

2 limes

salt, pepper

3 tbsp olive oil

Using a pair of heavy-duty scissors, snip the fins off the sea bass. With the back of a heavy knife, scrape off the scales and snip out the gills and eyes. Starting from the back of the head, follow the backbone with a sharp knife. Repeat on the underside until you reach the belly. Being careful not to cut through the flesh and make a hole, snip both ends of the backbone and pull it out. Remove the innards, remove the pin bones with a pair of tweezers and rinse clean. Dry the fish and keep it in the fridge until you're ready to cook it.

Put the rice in enough water to cover it twice over. Bring the water to the boil and cook the rice until tender – about 18 minutes. Drain well. Grill the pepper until charred all over. Peel off the blackened skin, remove the seeds and finely dice the flesh. Peel the shallots and chop three with the garlic. Sweat the shallots and garlic in a little olive oil until completely cooked but not coloured, then add the curry leaves, diced red pepper and chopped chilli to taste. Cook for 5 minutes, then add the rice and season with salt and pepper. Continue to cook, stirring well, for another 5 minutes, take off the heat and leave to cool. When the rice is cold, add some chopped coriander leaves and the juice of one lime.

Preheat the oven to 200°C/gas mark 6. Place the sea bass on a piece of lightly oiled greaseproof paper, season it and stuff with the rice mixture. Roll up the fish in the paper, twirling the ends so it's held nice and tight in the bag. Place on a heated baking tray in the preheated oven and cook for 8 minutes. Turn the bag over and continue to cook for 7 minutes. Bring to the table and open the bag to serve.

Accompany with a little vinaigrette made from 1 chopped shallot, the juice of 1 lime, chopped coriander leaves, salt and a tablespoon of olive oil. Season and, if you feel daring, add some more chilli.

Baked Cod 'Bourride Style'

SERVES 4

4 x 180g thick cod steaks

1 onion

4 sticks of celery

1 leek, white only

12 cloves of garlic

¼ head of celeriac, about 150g

1 bulb of fennel

1 large Desirée potato

a pinch of saffron

250ml dry white wine

1.5 litres of vegetable stock (see page 122)

4 tbsp olive oil

4 tbsp mixed chopped fresh herbs, such as tarragon, chervil, parsley and dill

salt, pepper

Clean, peel and roughly chop all the vegetables, keeping the potato separate. Put all except the potato in a large pan with a tablespoon of oil and stir and cook for 10 minutes until lightly coloured. Season well, add the saffron, potatoes and white wine. Reduce by half, then cover with the vegetable stock and simmer for 20 minutes. Blend and pass through a coarse sieve – this soup/sauce should be quite thick – and keep hot.

Preheat the oven to 220°C/gas mark 7. Place the cod steaks on a non-stick baking sheet, lightly brush them with olive oil and season. Cook for 7–8 minutes, depending on the thickness of the fish.

Ladle some hot soup into deep plates. Place a piece of cod in the centre and drizzle with the remaining olive oil mixed with chopped herbs.

Warm Poached Salmon with Caper and Parsley Vinaigrette

SERVES 4

4 x 160g salmon 'pavés', skin removed
juice of ½ a lemon
½ lemon, sliced
1 bay leaf
1 small bunch of thyme
2 shallots
½ bunch of flat-leaf parsley
½ bunch of curly parsley
1 tbsp superfine capers in vinegar
2 tbsp strong olive oil
salt, pepper

Place the pieces of salmon in a deep pan and cover with cold water. Add 2 slices of lemon, the bay leaf and thyme, and a generous amount of salt. Place over high heat and as soon as the water starts to boil, take the pan off the heat and loosely cover. The salmon will be perfectly cooked after 10 minutes.

Meanwhile, peel and chop the shallots, finely chop the washed curly parsley and coarsely chop the flat-leaf parsley. Drain the capers. Whisk the capers, shallots and parsley with the oil, lemon juice and 2 tablespoons of the salmon cooking liquid. Keep the vinaigrette sauce warm and serve with the fish.

Hamstring stretch

Women were barred from the first modern Olympics in 1896. British woman Violet Piercy was the first woman to run an officially timed marathon in 1926, when she completed the distance in three hours, 40 minutes and 22 seconds. But it was not until the 1988 Games that women finally ran an Olympic marathon.

Grilled Tuna and
Crushed White Beans with Pesto

SERVES 4

400–500g tuna loin, trimmed

160g dried butter beans

1 litre vegetable stock (see page 122)

60g dry-smoked bacon in one piece

2 cloves of garlic, peeled

1 tbsp olive oil

salt, pepper

Soak the white beans for 8–12 hours in plenty of water. Drain, cover with the vegetable stock and add the smoked bacon and garlic. Bring to the boil, skim, then turn down to a simmer. Cook for 30 minutes then season lightly and continue to cook until tender, topping up with water if necessary. Leave the beans to cool in their liquid.

Remove the bacon and chop very finely. Pan fry in a non-stick pan with a drizzle of olive oil until crispy. Drain the beans, keeping the cooking liquid, and crush them with the back of a fork. Add the bacon and enough of the cooking liquid to make the mixture moist but not sloppy.

Brush the tuna very lightly with olive oil and season well. Cook on a cast-iron griddle until rare or to your taste. Using a sharp knife, cut the tuna into slices and place on top of the beans. Take the remaining cooking liquid, bring to the boil, add 4 tablespoons of pesto and froth with a hand-held blender. To serve, rest the slices of tuna on a bed of beans and pour over the sauce.

Pesto

MAKES ABOUT 250ML

200g basil leaves

20g pine nuts

3 walnuts, roughly chopped

a pinch of salt

50g Parmesan cheese, freshly grated

150–200ml extra-virgin olive oil

Put the basil, nuts and salt in a large mortar and grind with a pestle to form a coarse paste. Work the Parmesan into the paste, then gradually beat in the olive oil with a wooden spoon until you have a thick sauce.

Alternatively, place all ingredients except the cheese (start with the smaller amount of oil) in a liquidizer or food processor and whizz briefly at high

speed. Add the cheese and blend for a few seconds. The secret of making pesto in a machine is not to overmix it; if the basil is blended for too long it will become hot and lose its bright green colour.

If you want the pesto for pasta, grilled fish or to garnish a soup, then keep it fairly coarse and dry. If it is for mixing into a sauce or to use as a salad dressing with a little balsamic vinegar, use more oil and blend until smooth. If stored in a clean airtight jar with a film of oil on top, pesto keeps in the refrigerator for up to 2 weeks.

Gravadlax

This recipe is for a whole salmon of about 5kg in weight, but you can reduce the quantities and prepare just one side of salmon or a smaller fish. The gravadlax can be wrapped in clingfilm and kept in the refrigerator for up to 10 days. Serve it cold in thin slices or cut it into big steaks and warm under a grill. It's vital to use really fresh, good-quality salmon – if you can afford it buy a wild fish. There is an organic salmon reared offshore in the Irish Sea on the market now. The quality is unbelievable – well worth looking out for.

1 x 5kg salmon, ask your fishmonger to scale and fillet the fish and remove the pin bones
20g coriander seeds
200g black and white peppercorns
6 star anise
15 cloves
1kg coarse sea salt
850g caster sugar
juice and zest of 2 lemons
juice and zest of 2 limes
4 bunches of fresh dill, about 100g
2 tsp dried dill
2 tsp English mustard

Gently rinse the salmon under cold water and dry well. Make 4 small incisions on the skin side of each fillet.

To make the marinade, break up the spices, using a spice mill or a mortar, and mix them with the salt, sugar and fruit juice and zest. Chop the dill, including the stalks, and add to the marinade.

Spread some of the marinade on to a flat stainless steel or plastic tray. Place a fillet skin side down in the pan and add a generous amount of the mix. Place the remaining fillet, skin side up, on top and pour over the remaining marinade. Cover with clingfilm and weigh down evenly with 1kg weights. Refrigerate for 8 hours then drain the liquid that has seeped from the fish, turn the fish over and weight it down again. Refrigerate for a further 8–12 hours, depending on how strong you like the cure.

When the fish is ready, drain off the marinade, brushing any off the fillets, and discard. Dry the fish with a clean towel, brush with a little English mustard and sprinkle with some dried dill.

Chicken with Walnut Sauce

SERVES 4

1 good-quality organic chicken

2 carrots

2 onions

3 cloves of garlic

1 leek

1 bunch of thyme

2 bay leaves

200g peeled walnuts made into a powder in a food processor

juice of ½ a lemon

salt, pepper, nutmeg

Peel the carrots, onions and garlic, wash the leek and chop them all roughly. Place in a deep pan with 3 litres of water, thyme, bay leaves and salt. If you have the neck, wings and feet of the chicken add them as well. Bring to the boil and skim, then simmer for 20 minutes before adding the whole chicken. Cook for 1¼ hours very gently – the stock should tremble or barely simmer. If the chicken is not submerged add a little hot water.

When the chicken is cooked, ladle out half a litre of the cooking liquid and reduce by half over a fierce heat. Whisk in the powdered walnuts and lemon juice and season with a little pepper and nutmeg.

To serve, carve the chicken into large pieces and ladle on some sauce. Perfect with pasta and braised celery hearts. Keep the rest of the stock for another recipe.

Warm Salad of Mussels
with Broad Beans and Mushrooms

SERVES 4

2.4kg small fresh live mussels

3 potatoes, Charlotte or similar

500g broad beans, unshelled weight

300g girolles

1 curly endive

1 tbsp red wine vinegar

2 tbsp olive oil

salt, pepper

Cook the potatoes in boiling salted water. Peel and slice them when they're cool enough to handle. Pod the broad beans and cook in boiling salted water. Refresh, drain and remove the tough outer skins of the beans.

Wash the mussels and put them into a scalding hot saucepan. Add 100ml of water and cover. Keep over a high heat, shaking the pan, until all the mussels have opened and are cooked. Pick them out of their shells, leaving a few in the shell for decoration.

Trim and clean the girolles. Only wash them if it's really necessary – simply wiping them with a damp cloth retains the flavour. Pan fry the girolles in a non-stick pan with a tiny drop of olive oil. When all the juices have evaporated, season and add the broad beans, mussels and potatoes. Reheat for a few seconds. Season with a vinaigrette made from 3 tablespoons of the mussel juice, 1 tablespoon of red wine vinegar and 2 tablespoons of olive oil. Toss the curly endive salad in the same dressing.

To serve, divide the mussel mixture between four plates and top with some endive salad and few mussels in their shells.

Grilled Mackerel with Green Asparagus and Anise-Flavoured Cauliflower Cream

SERVES 6

3 mackerel

30 medium-sized green asparagus spears

300g cauliflower

200ml milk

8 whole star anise

pastis

juice of 1 lemon

1 tbsp walnut oil

salt, pepper, olive oil

Fillet the mackerel and remove the pin bones with a pair of tweezers. Rinse and dry the fillets and cut into 12 equal diamonds. Peel the asparagus and cook in boiling salted water until almost done. Refresh in iced water and drain. Cut the cauliflower into florets and cook in salted boiling water. Refresh in iced water and drain. Bring the milk to the boil with the star anise and leave to cool. Pass the milk through a sieve, keeping the star anise to decorate the finished dish.

Keep back some florets for the garnish and put the rest of the cauliflower in a liquidizer or food processor. Blitz at full speed, slowly pouring in the sieved milk, until smooth. Season with salt, ground white pepper and a few drops of pastis and refrigerate until ready to use.

Toss the asparagus in the lemon juice, walnut oil, salt and pepper. Arrange the asparagus in a star on each plate with florets in between and put a generous spoon of cauliflower cream in the middle. Place the fillets of mackerel on a baking sheet, smear with olive oil and season with salt and pepper before placing under a hot grill to cook for 2–3 minutes. Place some mackerel on top of the cauliflower cream and serve immediately.

Venison Fillet with Pineapple Chutney and Vegetable Tagliatelle

SERVES 6

1.1kg trimmed venison loin

2 large carrots

2 courgettes

1 leek

2 shallots, chopped

2 tbsp red wine vinegar

1 tsp brown sugar

250ml veal stock (see page 123)

2 tbsp hazelnut oil

1 tbsp olive oil

salt, pepper

Peel and cut the carrots into tagliatelle-sized ribbons. Prepare the courgettes in the same way, but without peeling, and cut the leek into strips. Blanch the vegetables separately in salted boiling water, keeping them slightly crisp. Refresh in iced water and drain well.

Cut the venison into 18 equal 'noisettes'. Season them and pan fry in a non-stick pan with a drizzle of olive oil over high heat so that the meat is caramelized all over. The noisettes should take no more than 5–6 minutes to cook to medium-rare. Remove and keep warm.

Discard the fat in the pan and pour in the remaining olive oil. Add the chopped shallots and cook for 1 minute. Deglaze the pan with the vinegar and sugar. When it's almost dry, add the veal stock and boil until it has reduced by a third. Whisk in a tablespoon of hazelnut oil and check the seasoning. Reheat the vegetables in a non-stick pan with the remaining hazelnut oil and 2 tablespoons of water. Season well, then use a kitchen fork to make six twirls of vegetable, one for the middle of each plate. Add three 'noisettes', placing each one on a small spoonful of warm pineapple chutney. Drizzle some of the shallot sauce around the plate.

Pineapple Chutney

This recipe makes a lot more than is needed for the above dish, but it keeps for several months in an airtight jar in the refrigerator. Can be served with cold meats or other game.

1kg pineapple, peeled and cored weight

200g light brown sugar

300ml white wine vinegar

300g Bramley apples, peeled and grated

1 large onion, chopped

1½ chopped chillies

a pinch of pure saffron

2 tsp ground nutmeg

salt to taste

Cook the sugar, vinegar, apple, onion, chilli, saffron, nutmeg and salt in a heavy-based wide pan until syrupy. Add the pineapple cut into 2cm chunks, cover loosely and continue to cook, stirring occasionally, until translucent.

Rabbit with Mustard and Pastis

SERVES 4

1 whole rabbit (not wild)

1 onion

2 cloves of garlic

1 large bulb of fennel

2 tbsp Dijon mustard

260ml pastis

juice of 1 lemon

8 slices of smoked streaky bacon

1 bunch of fennel weed or dill

1 tbsp olive oil

salt, pepper

Joint the rabbit into 2 legs and 2 shoulders and cut the remaining body into 4 equal parts. Remove the lungs but keep the livers and kidneys. Your butcher should be able to do this for you, if not get another butcher! Peel and slice the onion and garlic. Cut the washed fennel into slices.

Rub the mustard on the rabbit pieces and place them in an ovenproof pan. Scatter in the vegetables and a little salt and pepper, add the pastis, oil and lemon, and cover with the bacon. Seal the pan with a tight-fitting lid and place in a moderate oven, 180°C/gas mark 4, for 20 minutes. Turn the oven down to 170°C/gas mark 3 and cook for a further 40 minutes. Take out of the oven to cool slightly but leave the lid on. Just before serving, sprinkle over the coarsely chopped fennel weed or dill.

This dish can also be made in advance and reheated. Don't worry about the alcohol content since it burns off during the cooking.

Chicken Supreme Tartlet
with Asparagus and Roquefort

SERVES 6

6 corn-fed chicken supremes

30 green asparagus spears, fewer if large

1 shallot

1 clove of garlic

100g oyster mushrooms

100g shiitake mushrooms

400ml vegetable stock (see page 122)

150g Roquefort cheese, broken into crumbs

1 tbsp walnut oil

1 tbsp olive oil

1 bunch of chervil

salt, pepper

Olive Oil Pastry

500g plain flour

50g olive oil

140g water

salt

To make the pastry, sieve the flour and salt. Tip on to a cold clean work surface and make a well in the centre. Using your fingertips, gradually add the oil and water to bring the paste together and gently shape it into a ball. Be careful not to overwork. Wrap in clingfilm and refrigerate for at least 2 hours before use.

Preheat the oven to 190°C/gas mark 5. Roll the pastry out to a thickness of 2mm and line six tartlet rings measuring about 9 x 2.5cm. Cover the pastry with greaseproof paper, add some dry beans and bake blind for 15 minutes. Leave to cool for a few minutes, then remove the beans and paper. Trim the rims of the tartlets and return them to the oven for 4–5 minutes to finish cooking.

Assembling the tartlets

Trim the asparagus and tie into bundles of ten. Cook in plenty of boiling salted water. Refresh in iced water and drain when cold. Trim to fit into the tartlets. Peel and chop the shallot and garlic. Clean and chop the mushrooms.

Season the chicken supremes and pan fry, skin-side down, in the olive oil until golden and crisp. Remove the chicken and tip out the oil and fat in the pan. Add the mushrooms, shallots and garlic and cook for 2 minutes, stirring with a spatula Add the chicken, skin-side up, and pour the vegetable stock into the pan. Simmer for 6–8 minutes until the chicken is cooked.

Remove the chicken and keep warm. Continue to cook the mushroom broth until it is reduced by half and the texture of thick soup. Using a hand-held blender, blitz until it is smooth and silky.

Reheat the asparagus in a steamer or warm oven and slice the chicken. Fill the tartlets with layers of chicken, asparagus, Roquefort cheese crumbs and mushroom sauce. Drizzle with walnut oil and decorate with chervil. Serve the tartlets warm with some more of the mushroom sauce on the side.

Chicken Supreme Grilled with Lemon and Garlic

SERVES 4

4 x 160g chicken supremes, skinned

2 cloves of garlic

2 tsp honey

1 tbsp olive oil

1 bunch of flat-leaf parsley

1 lemon, grated rind of ¼ and the rest cut into wedges

coarse sea salt

black pepper

Cut the wing bones off the supremes. Lay one supreme flat with the small fillet facing upwards. Slice the thickest part from the centre towards the outside, but do not cut off. Spread the supreme open, place between two sheets of thick plastic and flatten with a mallet until it is an even 1cm thick at the most. Repeat with the other three.

Chop the peeled garlic and mix with the honey, olive oil, chopped parsley and the grated rind of a quarter of the lemon. Smear this over the chicken supremes and refrigerate for 20 minutes before cooking. Cook the supremes on a cast-iron griddle for approximately 2 minutes each side.

Serve with a sprinkling of sea salt, coarsely ground black pepper and a wedge of lemon.

Minced Lamb with Preserved Lemon

SERVES 6

750g lean minced lamb

1 preserved lemon

1 large onion, peeled and finely chopped

½ tablespoon of olive oil

4 cloves of garlic, peeled and finely chopped

2 eggs

3 tsp ground cumin

a pinch of chilli powder

salt, pepper,

2 sprigs of rosemary, leaves stripped from stalks and chopped

vegetable stock (see page 122)

Cut the lemon in half and scoop out the flesh – it's not needed for this recipe. Finely chop the skin and add to the meat. Sweat the chopped onion with the olive oil until translucent, cool and add to the meat with the garlic, eggs, cumin and chilli powder. Season to taste. Beat the mixture well and shape into tight balls, the size of a golf ball. Heat a non-stick saucepan with a drop of olive oil, add the meatballs and seer on all sides. Add the rosemary, season and half cover the meat with vegetable stock. Bring to a gentle simmer and cook for 20 minutes, occasionally rolling the meatballs around in the pan. Serve with couscous and the broth. Alternatively, the meatballs can be grilled on thick rosemary stalks which have been stripped of their leaves.

Couscous

240g precooked couscous

6 plum tomatoes

3 spring onions

1 bunch of mint

cooking liquid from the minced lamb

2 tbsp golden raisins, blanched

salt, pepper

2 tbsp olive oil

Blanch and skin the tomatoes. Cut them in half and remove the seeds, then dry well and dice. Chop the spring onions and mint and set aside. Cook the couscous with the boiling cooking liquid from the meatballs, or, if grilling the meat, use water as instructed on the packet. Add the tomatoes, spring onions, mint, raisins and olive oil. Check the seasoning and serve warm.

Boiled Lamb Shanks with Star Anise Broth

SERVES 4

4 lamb shanks

1 onion, peeled and chopped

1 stick of celery, chopped

4 cloves of garlic, peeled and left whole

2 turnips

1 leek

12 star anise

salt and pepper

Trim 2cm from the tip of the bone of each lamb shank. This is mostly gristle and removing it makes the dish look better. Stand the shanks upright in a deep pan, add the chopped onion, celery, peeled whole garlic, washed and quartered turnips and star anise. Cover completely with water, season and put on a high heat. The shanks should be tightly packed in the pan.

Wash the leek, cut off the dark green top and add this to the lamb shanks. Cut the remaining leek in half, slice diagonally and set aside for later.

Once the lamb has come to the boil, skim and lower the heat to a very gentle simmer. The shanks should take about $1\frac{1}{4}$ hours to cook, but this varies depending whether it is young or old lamb. The meat should be tender, succulent and just about falling off the bone. Leave to cool for at least 1 hour in the stock, then drain through a fine sieve. This can be done the day before you want to eat the dish.

Handling the shanks carefully so as not to break them, place them in an flameproof dish. Pour over the broth, bring it to the boil and add the sliced leek. Cook for 5–6 minutes to reheat the shanks. Serve with boiled potatoes, turnips or swede.

Lamb Stew with Grapefruit and Chickpeas

SERVES 6

1.6kg neck end lamb chops (2 per person)

120g dried chickpeas

1 bay leaf

1 sprig of rosemary

2 large onions, peeled

200g button mushrooms

3 pink grapefruit

2 tbsp caster sugar

4 cloves of garlic

260ml fruity white wine

100ml vegetable or white chicken stock (see page 122)

3 tbsp olive oil

salt, pepper, nutmeg

Soak the chickpeas for 2–3 hours. Rinse well, cover generously with cold water, add the bay leaf and rosemary and bring to the boil. Skim and simmer for 45–60 minutes or until just tender.

Season the chops and sear in a non-stick pan with a little olive oil until well coloured on both sides. Set aside to drain off the fat. Add a little fresh oil to the pan and fry the peeled, sliced onions until golden brown. Put these in a colander to drain. Fry and drain the washed and sliced mushrooms.

Using a sharp, thin-bladed knife, peel the grapefruit, removing all the pith. Cut into segments and squeeze the juice from the remaining core and membrane. Take the peel of two of the grapefruit and cut into strips 5 x 50mm. Put the strips of peel into a pan, just cover with cold water and bring to the boil, then drain. Repeat twice. Put the peel back into the pan with the sugar and just enough water to cover. Bring to a gentle simmer and cook for 30 minutes, by which time the liquid should be quite syrupy.

Put the lamb in an ovenproof dish with the onions, mushrooms, chopped garlic, drained chickpeas, grapefruit juice, white wine, stock, cooked grapefruit peel with its syrup, and seasoning. Bring to a gentle simmer, cover loosely and cook in the oven at 180°C/gas mark 4 for 50–60 minutes. Any fat that rises to the surface is easily spooned off or poured away. Scatter over the grapefruit segments and serve piping hot.

Baked Ham and Spinach Pancakes

SERVES 6

12 pancakes

320g spinach

80g stale white bread, crusts off

120ml milk

4 shallots

1 tbsp olive oil

280g lean, good-quality cooked ham

80g Gruyère cheese, grated

salt, pepper, nutmeg

Wash the spinach well and blanch in boiling water for 30 seconds. Refresh in iced water, drain and squeeze until completely dry. Soften the bread in the milk and squeeze out any excess.

Sweat the chopped shallots in the olive oil until translucent and set aside to cool. Put the spinach, bread and ham through the fine blade of a mincer and mix well with a spatula Season with a little salt, pepper and nutmeg and fold in the shallots.

Preheat the oven to 200°C/gas mark 6. Set aside about a third of the filling mixture. Spread the rest over half of each pancake and fold in half. Spread the remaining mixture over half of each folded pancake and fold in half again to make triangular shapes. Place the pancakes in an ovenproof dish, sprinkle with the grated cheese and bake for 15–20 minutes. They should be glazed and crispy on the top and slightly puffed up. Serve immediately.

Pancakes

125g unbleached white flour

80g wholemeal flour

2 eggs

a pinch of salt

500ml milk

vegetable oil

Mix the eggs into the flour with a whisk. Add the milk gradually to avoid any lumps. Finally mix in the salt and leave the batter to rest for 60 minutes. Add a smear of vegetable oil to non-stick pan and cook the pancakes. This mixture should make more than 12 so allows for mishaps – and one for the cook. The pancakes should be very thin and well cooked, almost dry.

Calves' Liver with Wild Mushrooms and Sweet and Sour Onion

Athletes or anyone who trains regularly at a moderate to high intensity will automatically have an increased quantity of blood in the body. The reason for this is that the body has to makes more blood to help take enough oxygen to the hardworking muscles. But the body cannot make haemoglobin – the pigment in red blood cells that carries the oxygen – without iron, so we need to keep iron levels high. Iron supplements can have side effects and have to be taken with a good quantity of vitamin C to help absorption. A better option is to eat liver, lean meat, sardines, pulses and leafy vegetables.

SERVES 6

6 slices of calves' liver, 140g each

6 red onions

1 tbsp light muscovado sugar

2 tbsp sherry vinegar

200g oyster mushrooms

100g girolles

2 cloves of garlic

1 bunch of flat-leaf parsley

olive oil, salt, pepper

Peel and slice the onions. Put them in a wide, heavy-based pan with a drizzle of oil and sweat until lightly coloured. Add the sugar, salt and some coarsely ground pepper to taste and continue to cook over a medium heat, stirring to avoid burning. The sugar should caramelize fairly quickly. As soon as it has an amber colour, add the vinegar and partially cover. Lower the heat and cook for 30 minutes or until the onions have a soft, sweet, jammy consistency.

Trim and wash mushrooms if necessary – it's better just to wipe them with a damp cloth so they don't become laden with water. Cut the mushrooms into bite-size pieces and pan fry over fierce heat with a little olive oil until they are a light golden colour. Season. Just before serving, toss in the chopped garlic and parsley and cook for 20 seconds.

Lightly oil the liver and grill both sides for 3–4 minutes, depending on thickness, until it is cooked but still pink. Serve with the mushrooms and sweet and sour onions.

Sandra Petrou's Salt Beef

One of the most common causes of cramp for runners is an electrolyte imbalance in the body. Make sure to eat the recommended allowances of sodium, potassium and magnesium. Drinking plenty of fluids and stretching before and after running will also help alleviate cramps.

This recipe was given to me by my dear friend Sandra Petrou, a gourmet and a truly wonderful lady.

1 whole brisket of best quality beef (5.5–6kg)

500g coarse sea salt

250g demerara sugar

4 heaped tsp saltpetre

6 cloves of garlic, peeled and crushed

3 tsp pickling spice

3 tsp cracked white peppercorns

6 bay leaves

Mix the salt, sugar and saltpetre together and rub well into both sides of the meat. Put the meat into an earthenware or plastic dish and scatter on the rest of the ingredients and any leftover salt mix. Add cold water to cover and refrigerate for 10–12 days, turning daily.

To cook

Drain off the marinade and discard. Rinse the beef under cold water and place in a deep pan with just enough water to cover. Add 8 sugar cubes and 4 tablespoons of malt vinegar and bring to the boil. Skim and simmer for 4½–5 hours, topping up with hot water if necessary. A long wait for a great dish. Serve hot with mustard and boiled potatoes, or cold in a sandwich with relish, or with a baked potato.

Chicken Supreme with Pearl Barley Broth

This is a lovely winter warmer, filling and nourishing. It can be enhanced by a few drops of truffle oil just before serving or, better still, a liberal scattering of fresh black truffles.

SERVES 4

4 chicken supremes, each about 160g

2 sticks of celery

1 clove of garlic

1 leek

1 tbsp olive oil

600ml white chicken stock (see page 122)

120g pearl barley

parsley, tarragon, chervil, chopped

black truffle and/or truffle oil (optional)

salt, pepper

Peel the celery and cut into 6mm dice. Finely chop the garlic. Cut the leek in half, rinse under cold water and slice thinly, using the white and tender light green leaves.

Sweat the celery, garlic and leeks with the olive oil in a large saucepan. When they are soft, add the chicken stock and pearl barley, season lightly and bring to a simmer. Cook for 30 minutes or until the barley is tender – you may need to top up the liquid.

Drop the chicken supremes into the simmering broth, making sure they are submerged. Poach for 16 minutes or so, depending on the thickness of the supreme. Pour into deep plates and sprinkle with chopped herbs and the truffles or truffle oil if using.

Vegetable Stock

MAKES 2 LITRES

1 carrot

2 shallots

1 small onion

2 sticks of celery

1 leek (green top part only)

1 bay leaf

1 bunch of thyme

a handful of parsley stalks

Peel and roughly chop the vegetables and cover with about 2.5 litres of cold water. Add the herbs and bring to the boil. Simmer for 35 minutes, then strain.

White Chicken Stock

MAKES 4 LITRES

2kg chicken bones or wing tips

1 calf's foot, split

5 litres water

1 onion

1 small leek

2 sticks of celery

2 sprigs of thyme

6 parsley stalks

Place the bones and calf's foot in a large saucepan, cover with the water and bring to the boil. Skim off any fat and scum that come to the surface. Turn the heat down, add the remaining ingredients and simmer for 1½ hours, skimming occasionally.

Pass through a fine sieve and leave to cool. This stock can be kept in the refrigerator for up to 5 days or frozen.

Seafood Stock

MAKES ABOUT 2 LITRES

about 2kg of prawn, crab or lobster shells or scallop skirts

½ bulb of fennel

1 onion

1 bunch of basil

2.5 litres of water or enough to cover

2 tsp tomato paste

Chop the vegetables and basil, then put them in a large pan with the rest of the ingredients and bring to the boil. Skim and simmer for 25 minutes, then pass through a fine sieve. Keep in the refrigerator for 2–3 days or freeze.

Veal Stock

MAKES 3.5 LITRES

1.5kg veal bones, chopped and 1 calf's foot, split

1 tbsp olive oil

5 litres water

1 large onion

2 large carrots

1 stick of celery

2 cloves of garlic

2 sprigs of thyme

½ tbsp tomato purée

Roast the bones and calf's foot with the oil in a hot oven (220°C/gas mark 7), turning occasionally until brown all over, then put them into a large saucepan.

Roughly chop the onion, carrots and celery. Put into the roasting pan and roast until golden, turning frequently with a wooden spatula. Pour off any excess fat and add the roasted vegetables to the bones in the saucepan.

Put the roasting pan over a high heat and add 500ml of the water to deglaze the pan. Scrape the bottom with a wooden spatula to loosen all the caramelized sugars, then pour the liquid into the saucepan with the bones.

Add the remaining ingredients and bring to the boil. Skim off any scum and fat that come to the surface. turn down the heat and simmer gently for 3½ hours, skimming occasionally. Pass through a fine sieve and cool. This stock can be kept in the fridge for up to 10 days or frozen.

pasta, rice and pulses

Pasta Here are a few fresh pasta recipes that can easily be made at home with a hand roller – and a dustpan and brush to sweep up the flour that gets everywhere!

Obviously freshly made pasta is delicious, but so is the dried variety. Badly made pasta, fresh or dried, is repulsive. Many good delicatessens and supermarkets now stock fresh pasta and what you buy is down to trial and error and personal taste. My own preference is for egg-rich pasta and I shy away from 'flavoured' pasta, such as the bright green and red varieties. I would rather mix my spinach and tomatoes into a pasta as a sauce or eat them as a separate dish. Varieties of dried pasta made with different flours, such as spelt, kamut, rye and wholegrains, are far more interesting and then there are all the Asian varieties that are equally delicious. If you feel up to it after a long run in the park a few basic recipes follow. **Rice** Basmati, arborio, long-grain, wild Canadian, red Camargue to name but a few – they're all different but equally tasty. The staple food for around half the world's population, rice is gluten-free, so ideal for anyone with a wheat intolerance. **Pulses** All beans and pulses are rich in soluble fibre and a good-value carbohydrate food. A well-known English football star when asked about his diet that kept him in good shape replied 'chicken n' beans'. To this day the crowd show their adulation by shouting, 'We eat chicken n' beans' to this great player who never seems to tire.

Wholewheat Tagliatelle

SERVES 4

200g wholemeal flour

50g strong bread flour

3 egg yolks

1 whole egg

Put all the ingredients in a food processor and mix until combined, adding a few drops of water if necessary. Wrap the dough and leave to rest in the refrigerator for at least 1 hour. It should be pliable but not sticky.

Use a pasta machine to roll the dough out to the desired thickness. Cut the dough into tagliatelle strips and hang them over a clean broom handle held up on two chairs to dry. Once dry, put the strips on a lightly floured tray and cover with greaseproof. They keep in a dry cool place for up to a week. Cook in salted boiling water until al dente, drain and drizzle over a little olive oil.

Olive Oil and Whole Egg Tagliatelle

SERVES 4

400g plain white flour

30ml strong olive oil

4 whole eggs

pinch of salt

This dough is very pliable and can be made by hand without too much effort. Otherwise, prepare as above.

All-round Plain Pasta

SERVES 6

500g plain white flour

4 whole eggs

4 egg yolks

1 tbsp olive oil

pinch of salt

Prepare as wholewheat tagliatelle.

Quinoa and Broad Beans with Garlic and Coriander 'Pesto'

SERVES 4
250g shelled broad beans
120g quinoa
salt, pepper

Put the broad beans into boiling salted water and cook until tender – 3–4 minutes depending on size. Drain, then plunge them into iced water to halt the cooking and fix the green colour. Drain again and remove the tough skins to reveal the sweet kernels.

Boil the quinoa in 1½ times its volume of water until completely cooked. Use the directions on the packet, since cooking times vary depending on where the quinoa comes from. Don't let the pan dry out – the quinoa should still have a little moisture and the consistency of a risotto. Add the shelled broad beans and mix in some pesto to taste. Season with a generous amount of pepper and salt.

Garlic and Coriander 'Pesto'
12 cloves of garlic
2 big bunches of coriander (about 100g)
1 bunch of flat-leaf parsley
12 walnuts
8 tbsp olive oil
salt

This makes more than is needed for the quinoa recipe, but the pesto can be stored in an airtight container in the refrigerator for two weeks. Great with grilled fish, salads or simply on toast.

Peel the garlic cloves. Blend with the remaining ingredients until pastelike but not completely smooth. Be careful not to over-process or the pesto will loose its vibrant green colour. You can also make this pesto by hand with a pestle and mortar.

Wild Rice and Tiger Prawns

Wild rice has a particularly nutty flavour that goes well with seafood. This recipe uses tiger prawns but it can be prepared with langoustines, lobster, squid, scallops or a combination of these. Serve as a starter or to accompany any fish dish, or increase the quantities and serve by itself as a main course.

SERVES 6

360g wild rice

18 tiger prawns

2 small onions, finely chopped

1 red pepper, peeled and diced

1 yellow pepper, peeled and diced

butter

1 litre of seafood stock (see page 123)

salt and pepper

Preheat the oven to 160°C/gas mark 3. Rinse the rice in cold water and drain well. Sweat the onions and peppers with a tablespoon of butter in an ovenproof pan until soft. Add the rice and continue to cook, stirring, for 2 minutes. Pour in 600ml of stock and bring to the boil. Cover the pan with greaseproof paper and place in the oven for about 40 minutes. Stir every 15 minutes, adding a little more stock if needed. At the end of the cooking time the rice should have absorbed all the liquid, be tender and just starting to crack open. Season and fluff up the rice with a little butter.

Remove the heads of the prawns, then shell them leaving the tail intact. Keep the shells and heads for stock. With a sharp knife, slit down the back of each prawn to remove the entrails and open out the prawn. Grill or pan fry in a non-stick pan smeared with olive oil. Season the prawns and serve them with the rice.

Tagliatelle with Green Olive Paste and Bayonne Ham

SERVES 4

300g dried tagliatelle

8 slices of Bayonne Ham (or air-dried ham such as Parma)

salt, pepper

Shred the ham. Boil the pasta until al dente in plenty of boiling, salted water. Drain, toss in the olive paste and add the shreds of ham. Serve immediately, with freshly ground pepper.

Olive Paste

100g good-quality green olives (not in brine)

2 red peppers

5 tbsp olive oil

1 tbsp of thyme leaves picked off the stems, plus a few sprigs for decoration

Remove the olive stones. Char, skin and dice the peppers. Blend the olives with the oil until pastelike but not smooth. Mix in the peppers and thyme. This makes more you need for the pasta, but it keeps well in the fridge.

Penne with Lemon and Parsley

SERVES 4

320g penne pasta

1 large lemon

2 tbsp pine nuts, toasted

4 spring onions, thinly sliced

4 tbsp olive oil

1 bunch of flat-leaf parsley, washed and coarsely chopped

salt, pepper

Peel half the washed lemon, making sure you have only the yellow skin not the pith. Cut the skin into very fine julienne strips and boil and drain them twice. Juice the lemon and set aside. Boil the pasta in plenty of salted water, drain and rinse in warm water. Return the pasta to the pan with the olive oil, salt, pepper, toasted pine nuts and spring onions and toss over the heat for a minute or two. Add the parsley and lemon juice and rind, then serve at once.

Tagliatelle with Green Olive Paste and Bayonne Ham (*opposite*)

Almond Basmati Rice Scented with Cinnamon

SERVES 4

200g basmati rice

2 cloves of garlic

½ onion

1 tbsp olive oil

1 stick of cinnamon and some ground cinnamon for dusting

1 tsp caster sugar

400ml vegetable stock (see page 122)

60g flaked almonds

1 tbsp butter (optional)

salt, pepper

The quantity of liquid needed may vary depending on the basmati rice used, so check the instructions on the packet.

Peel and chop the onion and garlic and sweat in an heatproof casserole with the olive oil until tender but not coloured. Add the cinnamon stick and sugar, then pour on the vegetable stock and rice. Lightly season and bring to the boil for one minute. Seal the pan with a tight-fitting lid, take it off the heat and leave for 30 minutes without removing the lid. The rice should have absorbed all the liquid and be perfectly cooked.

Lightly toast the almonds under a grill and fork them into the rice with a little butter if you like. Dust with a little ground cinnamon before serving.

The first London Marathon was held in March 1981. There were 7,747 runners and 6,255 reached the finish line. Since then, the London Marathon has taken place every year and 508,352 runners have completed the course.

Asparagus and Parmesan Risotto

SERVES 4

200g arborio rice

24 asparagus spears

400ml vegetable stock (see page 122)

1 onion

1 tbsp butter

60ml dry white wine

60g Parmesan shavings

1 tbsp mascarpone cheese

salt, pepper

Peel the asparagus spears and tie them into bundles of six. Cook in salted boiling water until tender, then refresh in iced water to halt the cooking and fix the colour. Drain and cut off the tips 3cm down. Put the stalks in a liquidizer or food processor with the vegetable stock and blitz to a purée. Pass this through a fine sieve and set aside.

Chop the onion and sweat in half of the butter until soft. Stir in the rice and continue to cook for another 2 minutes. Pour the wine on to the rice and cook until it is all absorbed.

Add the asparagus stock to the rice a ladleful at a time, stirring occasionally. Keep it simmering gently for 18–20 minutes by which time the rice should have absorbed all the liquid and be cooked. Take off the heat and fold in the mascarpone and remaining butter. Season well and add the asparagus tips and Parmesan shavings. Serve immediately.

Hip stretch

Butter Beans with Chorizo and Tomato

I adore pulses and pasta and can quite happily eat them instead of meat or fish as the main component of a meal. Pulses are delicious dressed with 'Fleur de Sel' or coarse sea salt, olive oil and lemon juice and served as a salad with a main course or as a complete and satisfying meal. Try mixing pulses with strong flavours such as anchovies, smoked meats or sausages – a little will go a long way.

SERVES 4

200g dried butter beans (320g for main course; increase the other ingredients accordingly)

12 thin slices of spicy dry chorizo

1 bay leaf

2 sprigs of thyme

6 plum tomatoes

4 shallots

1 clove of garlic

3 tbsp olive oil

1 bunch of flat-leaf parsley

salt, pepper

Soak the butter beans in cold water for 2 hours. Drain and put in a pan with fresh water to cover by at least 6cm and add the bay leaf and thyme. Bring to the boil, skim and reduce the heat to a gentle simmer. After 30 minutes add salt and continue to cook for 45–60 minutes until tender.

Meanwhile blanch the tomatoes, skin, cut in half and remove the seeds. Chop the tomato flesh roughly and set aside. Peel and chop the shallots and garlic, then sweat with 1 tablespoon of olive oil until tender but not browned. Add the tomato, season well and continue to cook gently for 15–20 minutes, until you have a pulpy tomato sauce.

Drain the beans when they are cooked. If you don't like the thick skin of butter beans now is the time to remove them. Otherwise, gently fold the beans into the tomato sauce. Add the remaining olive oil and fold in the washed and coarsely chopped parsley. Turn everything into a heatproof serving dish and scatter the chorizo slices on top. Place under a grill for 2 minutes so that the chorizo weeps some of its delicious juices into the beans. Serve warm.

Chickpeas with Saffron and Coriander

The chickpeas need to be soaked overnight, so start this recipe the day before.

SERVES 4

240g dried chickpeas

2 lemons

1 stick of celery

2 cloves of garlic

1 bunch of coriander, remove the leaves from the stalks

80g golden raisins

6 shallots

2 pinches of pure saffron strands

2 red peppers

1 red chilli

4 tsp olive oil

salt, pepper

Peel one of the lemons and cut the peel into very thin julienne strips. Blanch in salted water and rinse. Repeat three times. Juice both lemons and set aside.

Drain the soaked chickpeas, rinse and put in a pan with fresh water to cover. Add the celery stick, the peeled garlic and the coriander stalks and bring to the boil. Skim, then simmer for 30 minutes. Add salt and continue to cook for 45–60 minutes until tender. Leave to cool in the water until cool enough to handle and remove the tough skins – my grandmother swears that removing the skin prevents the nasty side effect these peas can cause!

Drain and remove the celery and coriander stalks. The garlic should have disintegrated. Blanch the raisins for 1 minute, drain and add them to the chickpeas with the lemon peel.

Slice the shallots and pan fry in a little olive oil until golden brown. Add half the lemon juice and the saffron and cook for 20 seconds. Pour this mixture into a serving dish with the chickpeas. Fold in the coarsely chopped coriander leaves, season and drizzle with a little olive oil.

Put the peppers under a hot grill until black all over. When cool enough to handle, peel off the skin and remove the core and seeds. Blend the flesh with the chilli (with or without seeds depending how spicy you want it) and the rest of the olive oil and lemon juice until smooth, adding a little of the chickpea cooking liquid if needed to make into a sauce. Season and pour this sauce around the chickpeas. Best served warm.

Spaghetti with Razor Clams, Parsley and Garlic

Make sure your razor clams are alive and bought from reputable fishmonger. If you can't get razor clams, use a mixture of clams such as Venus, Surf, Amande or Palourde.

SERVES 4

300g dried spaghetti

1kg fresh live razor clams

2 shallots

200ml dry white wine

1 bunch of flat-leaf parsley, chopped

2 cloves of garlic, peeled and chopped

1 or 2 red chillies to taste, chopped

4 tbsp olive oil

salt, pepper

Rinse the razor clams in cold water. Finely chop the shallots and sweat in a large saucepan with half a tablespoon of olive oil. Add the clams and turn up the heat. Pour in the wine and cover tightly. After 3 or 4 minutes, shake the pan and check the clams. The exact time they take to cook will depend on the variety used. As soon as all the clams are open, take the pan off the heat – they go chewy if overcooked. Drain into a colander set over a bowl so you collect all the juices. Pick out the flesh of the clams – leave a few in their shells for decoration – and remove the little sand bag or intestine at the base of each meaty mollusc. Pass the cooking juices through a fine sieve and boil until reduced by half.

Cook the pasta in plenty of boiling, salted water, drain and put back in the pan. In another pan reheat the clams in the reduced juice and add the oil, chopped parsley, garlic and chillies. Pour this mixture into the pasta and toss everything together. Check for seasoning, decorate each bowl with some clams in the shell and serve immediately.

Green Lentils
and Warm Potatoes with Anchovies

This can be served as a starter, main course or even as a side salad to go with a grilled fish. The most important point in this recipe is the quality of the anchovies. They must not be oversalted or they will loose their delicate taste; they should also be firm, fleshy and resemble fish, not brown slivers of cardboard. Double the quantities if serving as a main course.

SERVES 4

200g green Puy lentils

8 anchovy fillets

4 medium Charlotte or Belle de Fontenay potatoes

1 carrot

2 shallots

½ leek

140ml vegetable stock (see page 122)

2 tbsp red wine vinegar

3 tbsp of olive oil

1 bunch of flat-leaf parsley

salt, pepper

Rinse the lentils in cold water. Put them in a saucepan, generously cover with water and set over a high heat. Bring to the boil, skim and simmer until the lentils are tender, usually about 40 minutes. Drain, discard the cooking liquid and keep the lentils warm.

Wash the potatoes and cook them in their skins in salted boiling water. When cool enough to handle, peel off the skins, cut the potatoes in half and keep warm with the lentils.

Peel and finely chop the carrot, shallots and leek and put them in a wide pan with the stock. Simmer until tender, stirring occasionally. Fold in the lentils, season lightly with salt and generously with pepper, then add the oil, vinegar and chopped parsley. Serve warm with the anchovy fillets cut into strips and draped over the potatoes.

Black Kidney Beans
with Fennel Seed and Red Peppers

SERVES 4

160g dried black kidney beans

3 red peppers

1 tbsp fennel seeds

2 medium red onions

2 cloves of garlic

3 tbsp olive oil

150ml vegetable stock (see page 122)

1 tbsp red wine vinegar

salt, pepper

Soak the kidney beans in cold water overnight. The next day, drain the beans, put them in a pan and cover generously with cold water. Bring to the boil for at least 10 minutes to ensure the removal of poisonous toxins. Turn down the heat and simmer for 40–50 minutes or until tender.

Grill the peppers until their skins have turned black. Cover with clingfilm and leave to cool. When they're cool enough to handle, peel off the blackened skin, remove the seeds and cores and cut the flesh into large dice.

Peel and chop the onions and pan fry in a non-stick pan with half a table-spoon of olive oil until tender. Add the chopped garlic, peppers and fennel seeds and continue to cook for 2–3 minutes.

Drain the beans and crush them with a fork so that about half of them are broken up but just holding together. Add them to the frying pan with the vegetable stock and red wine vinegar and season well. When everything is piping hot, drizzle over the rest of the oil and serve. This dish is also good eaten cold as a salad.

vegetables and salads

French Bean and Wet Walnut Salad

Wet walnuts are the new season's crop. They're still wet and haven't been through the drying process that preserves them. Much more delicate than the dry versions, they are milky in taste with none of the bitterness that can be associated with walnuts. They are usually available from late September until mid-November, depending on the country or region they come from.

SERVES 4

480g fine french beans

20 fresh wet walnuts

1 shallot, chopped

salt, pepper

2 tbsp walnut oil

2 tbsp red wine vinegar

chervil

Top and tail the french beans. Blanch them in plenty of boiling, salted water until tender but still with a little 'bite'. Plunge into ice-cold water to keep their vibrant green colour and halt the cooking. Drain well and season with the oil, vinegar, chopped shallot, salt and pepper.

Crack the walnuts, pick out the kernels and scatter them over the salad with a generous amount of chopped chervil.

Groin stretch

The first New York Marathon took place in September 1970 with only 127 runners. Now 30,000 people take part each year, watched by millions of spectators.

Ratatouille

A wonderful dish in its own right, this can be served as a main course with the addition of a poached egg and some cured ham. It is excellent served with roast lamb or as a cold salad with a few leaves of basil and a drizzle of strong olive oil added at the last minute.

SERVES 6

6 red peppers

4 green peppers

1 large onion

2 courgettes

2 aubergines

2 cloves of garlic

4 plum tomatoes and 1 tsp tomato paste

2 sprigs of thyme

1 bay leaf

olive oil

salt, pepper

Peel the peppers with a peeler. Cut them into quarters, remove the seeds and cut into 1cm dice. Peel the onion and cut into similar-sized pieces. Peel and crush the garlic. Wash and dice the courgettes, keeping the skin but avoiding the centre seeded part if soft, and prepare the aubergines the same way. Blanch and skin the tomatoes, de-seed and dice.

Heat a non-stick pan and smear with olive oil. Pan fry the courgettes, onions, peppers and aubergine separately until golden in colour, placing each in a colander to drain as you go. Let them drain for 10 minutes, then put all the ingredients into a heavy-based saucepan or casserole. Season well and bring up to a simmer, stirring occasionally to avoid burning. Lower the heat, cover with a lid and cook for 25 minutes or until all the vegetables are soft.

Watercress and Pear Salad, with Sweet Mustard Dressing

SERVES 6

6 bunches of watercress, about 80g per person

1 red onion

2 William pears

pepper

Make the mustard dressing. Cut off and discard the thickest parts of the watercress stalks. Wash the rest well in ice-cold water, drain and spin dry. Peel and thinly slice the onion. Peel the pear and slice into paper-thin curls with a Japanese vegetable slicer or a peeler. Be sure to do this at the last moment or the pear will discolour. Gently toss all the ingredients together with the mustard dressing and season well with pepper.

Sweet Mustard Dressing

1 tbsp scented honey

1 tbsp malt vinegar

2 tbsp wholegrain mustard

a pinch of salt

4 tbsp olive oil

Whisk the honey, vinegar, salt and mustard together, then gradually whisk in the oil. This recipe makes more than enough for the above salad, but the dressing can be stored for several weeks.

Heart of Cos Lettuce with Aged Mimolette Cheese and Truffles

SERVES 4

1 cos lettuce

1 or 2 fresh Périgord truffles (*Tuber melanosporum*)

4 tbsp olive oil

1 clove of garlic

1 tbsp red wine vinegar

120g aged mimolette cheese

1 bunch of chervil, leaves picked from the stems

16 very thin croutons cut from a thin baguette

salt, pepper

Toast the croutons, rub them with half the garlic clove and drizzle sparingly with olive oil. Trim the lettuce, keeping only the heart, and wash and spin dry. Using a peeler or a cheese knife, cut shavings of mimolette cheese.

Toss the lettuce in a large bowl with a little salt, pepper, half a clove of pressed garlic, the remaining olive oil and red wine vinegar. When it is well coated, gently fold in the cheese and croutons. Finally, shave the truffles over the salad and add the chervil leaves. Serve in a big bowl or divide on to plates.

You can also make mimolette crisps to decorate the salad. Finely grate 160g of mimolette cheese and spread it 2–3mm thick on a baking mat in any shape you want. Grill until the cheese looks cooked and golden. Leave it to cool for 20 seconds, then scape it off and leave to set on a dry, flat surface.

Boston is the oldest of the yearly city marathons. The first race was run on 19 April 1897 and was won by John J. McDermott of New York. Fifteen runners took part.

Cheese and Smoked Bacon Potato

This makes a delicious garnish for a simple main course such as grilled meat.

SERVES 6

6 large Charlotte or similar potatoes, about 5cm long

2 tbsp crème fraîche

260g smoked Alsace belly pork, pancetta or strong smoked streaky bacon

120g mature cheddar, grated

pepper, salt, nutmeg

Wash the potatoes, but do not peel them, and cook in boiling, salted water. Drain. Take a very small slice off along the length of a potato so it sits firmly without rolling over. Take a 6–8mm slice off the top and gently and carefully remove some of the potato flesh, without breaking the skin, to form a boat. Repeat with the other five. Put all the scooped-out potato into a bowl and crush with the crème fraîche, salt, pepper and nutmeg.

Preheat the oven to 200°C/gas mark 6. Blanch the belly pork and cut off 6 very fine slices. Chop the remaining belly finely and add to the potato mix. If you're using bacon, keep aside 6 slices and chop the rest as for the belly pork. Fill the boats with the mixture, top with grated cheese and bake for 12–15 minutes until golden brown. While the potatoes are cooking, grill the slices of belly pork or bacon until crispy and add them to the tops of the potatoes before serving.

Hip flexor stretch

Braised Celery Hearts

SERVES 6

6 celery hearts (about 200g each)

1 medium onion

2 large carrots

3 bay leaves

1 bunch of curly parsley, chopped

800ml vegetable stock (see page 122)

juice of 1 lemon

3 tbsp olive oil

salt, pepper

Peel the onion and carrots. Cut the onion in four then slice across. Slice the carrots into 3mm discs and set aside. In a pan wide enough to take the celery hearts heat a tablespoon of olive oil. Cook the onions until lightly coloured, add the carrots and continue to cook, stirring occasionally, for another 3–4 minutes. Place the celery hearts on top of the onions and carrots and sprinkle with the chopped parsley, bay leaves, salt and a generous amount of pepper. Add the vegetable stock and bring to the boil. Reduce the heat, cover loosely and simmer for 20–25 minutes, turning occasionally.

Before serving, remove the vegetables from the pan with a slotted spoon and boil the remaining liquid until it is reduced by half. Add the lemon juice, pour the liquid over the vegetables and drizzle with the remaining olive oil.

Savoy Cabbage and Grain Mustard

SERVES 6

1 Savoy cabbage

1 medium onion

3 cloves of garlic

2 tbsp wholegrain mustard

1 tbsp peppery olive oil

juice of 2 lemons

salt, pepper

Peel and thinly slice the onion and garlic. Remove the dark outside leaves of the cabbage and cut it into four. Remove the core from each piece and thinly slice. In a wide, heavy-based pan, lightly caramelize the onions with the olive oil. Add the garlic and cabbage and cook over a moderate heat, stirring occasionally. Season well, partially cover and cook for 12–15 minutes until just tender. Pour in the lemon juice and fold in the mustard. Serve hot or cold.

Braised Little Gem Lettuces

SERVES 6

6 little gem lettuces

2 shallots

1 carrot

1 stick of celery

1 tbsp of thyme leaves picked from the stems

2 tbsp olive oil

1 tbsp of light muscovado sugar

salt, pepper

100ml port

250ml veal stock (see page 123) or chicken stock (see page 122)

Some little gems are sold ready washed. If not, remove the the outer leaves of the lettuces, put the hearts under cold running water and shake dry.

Peel and chop the shallots, carrot and celery very, very finely. Add the thyme leaves. Put some oil in a wide, thick-based pan over very high heat. When it's smoking hot, add the gems and colour on all sides. Add the other vegetables, salt, pepper and sugar, shake the pan and lower the heat to a medium flame.

After 6 minutes, pour on the port and simmer for 10 minutes, turning the gems twice. Add the veal stock and continue to cook and turn the lettuces until the liquid has become syrupy.

Serve immediately with grilled liver or other meats. This dish can also be cooled and kept for several days in the refrigerator. Reheat when needed.

Tunisian Grilled Vegetable Salad

SERVES 6

6 plum tomatoes

juice of 2 lemons

a pinch of saffron

2 tsp cumin seeds

½ tsp harissa

2 cloves of garlic, chopped

12 new season onions

3 green peppers

3 red peppers

1 large courgette

2 aubergines

2 tbsp olive oil

1 bunch of coriander

salt, pepper

Blanch the tomatoes in boiling water, refresh in iced water and skin. Cut them in half and chop roughly. In a scalding hot, non-stick pan, cook the tomato flesh for 2 minutes until it becomes pulpy. Add the seasoning, lemon juice, saffron, cumin seeds, harissa and chopped garlic, take off the heat and whisk in the olive oil.

Cut the new season onions in half and grill on a cast-iron griddle, leaving them slightly crunchy. Roast the peppers under a hot grill until blackened all over, cover with clingfilm and leave to cool. When cool, peel off the black skin, remove the stalk, core and seeds, and cut into wide strips.

Cut the courgette and aubergine into 6mm slices and grill on both sides. Leave to cool. Season the cold vegetables and arrange on plates with a little of the tomato dressing in between. Garnish with the fresh coriander.

Celeriac and Sultana Salad with Harissa

SERVES 4

400g celeriac

2 tbsp golden sultanas

1 clove of garlic

100ml vegetable stock (see page 122)

salt

harissa to taste

2 tsp tomato paste

juice of 2 limes

2 tbsp olive oil (thick, strong variety)

1 bunch of mint, chopped

1 bunch of coriander, chopped

Peel the celeriac. Cut into fine julienne strips with a Japanese vegetable slicer or grate on a fine grater. Put the sultanas in a pan with cold water, bring to the boil for 30 seconds and drain. Peel and crush the garlic, place it in a mortar or blender. Slowly add the vegetable stock, salt, tomato paste, harissa, lime juice and olive oil, mixing or blending until smooth.

Pour this dressing over the celeriac and raisins, toss well and refrigerate. Leave to marinate for at least 2–3 hours. Just before serving, fold in some chopped coriander and mint leaves.

Mangetout with Garlic and Shiitake Mushrooms

SERVES 4

160g mangetout, topped and tailed

4 cloves of garlic

160g shiitake mushrooms

juice of ½ a lime

2 tbsp olive oil

1 tsp sesame oil

salt, pepper

Blanch the mangetout in salted boiling water, making sure to keep them crisp and underdone. Refresh in iced water and drain well. Thinly slice the peeled garlic, removing any green stem inside. Slice the shiitake mushrooms to the same thickness as a mangetout

In a non-stick pan over high heat, cook the mushrooms with half the olive oil until slightly coloured but still undercooked. Leave the heat high, add the mangetout and garlic, season and keep stirring. The whole process should take not more than 3 minutes. Serve the salad immediately, drizzled with the remaining oil and the lime juice.

Chicken Liver and Baby Spinach Salad

SERVES 4

240g chicken livers

260g baby spinach, washed

1 red, 1 green and 1 yellow pepper

12 white seedless grapes

2 tsp white wine vinegar

3 tbsp olive oil

2 spring onions, sliced

salt, pepper

Make sure the chicken livers are fresh – frozen ones tend to break-up while cooking. Drain them well, dry on paper towels and trim off any nerves and parts with a greenish-yellow colour. These have been in contact with the bile and may be bitter.

Peel the peppers with a peeler, remove the cores and seeds. Lay the flesh flat then cut into a fine julienne strips. Smear a non-stick pan with oil and pan fry the peppers with salt and pepper until soft. Set aside and keep warm. Squash the grapes through a fine sieve and add the vinegar.

Pan fry the seasoned chicken livers in the non-stick pan with a tiny drop of olive oil. When golden on both sides but still pink inside, remove them from the pan. Discard any fat from the pan, pour in the grape juice and boil for 1 minute. Take the pan off the heat and whisk in the remaining olive oil and vinegar. Season the spinach leaves, then toss them with the grape juice vinaigrette. Add the warm peppers and sliced spring onion to the spinach and finally the chicken livers. Serve immediately.

Endive and Poached Egg
Salad with Red Onions and Dry-Cured Bacon

Red onions can be a wonderful addition to most recipes, but did you know that chewing raw onion for three to eight minutes leaves the lining of the mouth completely sterile? It also enables you to get to the front of the start line, no questions asked!

SERVES 6

6 eggs

12 very thin slices of ventreche (air-dried bacon) or pancetta

4 Belgian endives

2 red onions

18 walnuts

1 tbsp water

4 tbsp balsamic vinegar

6 tbsp olive oil

salt, pepper

Place the walnuts in a blender with the water, vinegar, olive oil, salt and pepper and blitz to make the vinaigrette. Leave it fairly grainy so you keep some of the crunch of the walnuts.

Crack the eggs into separate cups and gently pour them into unsalted boiling water with a generous amount of vinegar. Cook for no more than 3 minutes for soft eggs. Remove them with a slotted spoon and gently place in iced water to halt the cooking. Drain and trim the edges with a pair of scissors. Dry carefully and wrap each egg in two slices of ventreche.

Cut the endives at the base to release all the leaves. Arrange the smaller leaves in a circle around each plate and thinly slice the rest to put in the middle. Peel the onions, cut into thin rings and intersperse with the endive. Drizzle an equal amount of walnut vinaigrette on to each plate. To reheat the eggs, place them in a lightly oiled dish and warm in a preheated oven (200°C/gas mark 6) for 4–5 minutes. Put an egg in the centre of each plate and serve.

Endive and Dandelion Salad with Scallops

These are both bitter leaves, but here they are served with a sweet dressing and scallops, which contrast with and enhance them. Dandelions grow almost all year round in Europe, but are best in autumn or winter. Pick the smallest leaves which are tender and not so bitter. Particularly high in iron and potassium, dandelions are also a diuretic hence their French name 'pissenlit' which translates as 'wet the bed'.

SERVES 6

18 scallops

6 heads of dandelion leaves

2 red endives

2 yellow endives

2 shallots, chopped

1 Granny Smith apple

12 red radishes

2 tbsp honey

2 tbsp sherry vinegar

60ml veal stock (see page 123) or chicken or vegetable stock (see page 122)

2 tbsp hazelnut oil

salt, pepper, olive oil

Pick over the dandelion leaves and wash well. Separate the endive into leaves. Peel and finely chop the shallots. Cut the apple into matchsticks and sprinkle them with a little lemon juice and water to stop them going brown. Slice the radishes. Trim the scallops and pat them dry with kitchen towel.

Heat a non-stick pan and smear the base with olive oil. When it's smoking hot, sear the seasoned scallops on both sides until golden outside and still 'pink' inside. This should take 60–90 seconds each side depending on the thickness of the scallops and the fierceness of the heat. Remove the scallops from the pan and keep warm.

Put the pan back over high heat and add the chopped shallots. Toss them around for 30 seconds until just starting to caramelize. Add the honey and continue to cook for a further 30 seconds. Then deglaze the pan with the vinegar, add the stock and bring to the boil for 45 seconds. Take off the heat, whisk in the hazelnut oil and season. Use this vinaigrette to dress the salad, keeping some back to drizzle on each serving. To serve, place some endive salad on each plate and top with scallops and dandelions leaves. Decorate with batons of apple and radish slices and drizzle over the rest of the vinaigrette.

Warm Leek, Potato and Tomato Salad with Carrot Juice Dressing

SERVES 4

1 large leek

4–6 Charlotte potatoes

2 beef or marmande tomatoes

3 or 4 carrots, enough to make 100ml of juice

juice of 1 lemon

3 tbsp olive oil

salt, pepper

If you have a vegetable juicer, prepare the carrot juice and keep it cold. If you don't, finely grate the peeled carrots, season and add a few drops of lemon juice. Cover and refrigerate for 4 hours, then squeeze though a very fine sieve. Alternatively, buy 100ml of carrot juice in a juice bar or supermarket.

Wash the potatoes and cook them in their skins in salted water. When they are cool enough to handle, peel and slice. Season with salt, pepper and a drizzle of olive oil and lemon juice, then cover and keep warm. Cut the leek in half, then thinly slice it across. Wash the slices well and cook in boiling salted water until just done. Refresh in iced water and drain well.

Remove the cores of the tomatoes and cut across into 6mm slices. Sear in a scalding-hot, non-stick pan for 10 seconds on both sides. Shape each serving in a metal ring, 6–8cm across: arrange a bed of leeks, followed by warm potatoes lightly seasoned with salt and pepper, tomatoes and finally more leek. Remove the ring. Serve warm, decorated with a fine julienne of carrot. Dress with the carrot vinaigrette made by mixing the juice with the remaining olive oil, lemon juice, salt and pepper.

Oriental Summer Salad

SERVES 4

1 grapefruit

4 spring onions

12 red radishes

¼ Savoy cabbage

1 carrot

1 round lettuce

160g bean sprouts

1 tbsp crunchy peanut butter

1 tbsp each of light soy sauce, clear honey and sesame oil

juice of 1 lime

salt, pepper

With the back of a fork, mix the honey and peanut butter together, gradually adding the lime juice, soy sauce and sesame oil. Check the seasoning and set aside.

Peel the grapefruit and separate into segments. Slice the spring onions and radishes. Shred the cabbage and blanch in boiling, salted water for 10 seconds Refresh, drain and dry well. Peel the carrot and cut into very fine julienne strips. Put these in iced water to curl for an hour.

Just before serving, toss the vegetables in the dressing and serve in the leaves of the round lettuce. Decorate with the grapefruit segments and the drained carrot julienne.

desserts

Muscovado sugar is used in most of my recipes because it brings another dimension to the taste of the dessert.

The sugar content is slightly reduced, yet the intensity and complexity of taste increases. Caramel, coffee and hints of aniseed are just some of the notes that this king of sugars bring to the palate. I have been known in moments of weakness to eat muscovado by the spoonful.

Compote of Banana and Orange with Vanilla and Muscovado Sugar

Muscovado sugar comes in various colours and degrees of stickiness. For this recipe it's best to use a light muscovado, so as not to overpower the vanilla.

SERVE 4

4 bananas

6 oranges

75g caster sugar

2 vanilla pods

120g muscovado sugar

30ml dark rum

Peel two of the oranges and cut the peel into fine julienne. Juice the oranges and set aside. Cover the strips of peel with cold water and bring to the boil. Strain and repeat three times. Cover with a syrup made with 100ml water and 75g caster sugar, bring to the boil and simmer for 30 minutes or until tender. Peel the remaining oranges with a sharp knife, divide them into segments and set aside. Press the remaining core and membrane to collect all the juice and add this to the juice set aside earlier. Put the juice in a pan with the split vanilla pods, rum and half the sugar. Boil and reduce by one third.

Peel the bananas, slice and add to the juice. Simmer, stirring with a wooden spoon, until lightly cooked. Pour the banana compote into bowls and arrange the orange segments on top. Sprinkle over the remaining sugar and glaze under a hot grill or with a blow torch. Decorate with the orange-peel confit.

Nutty Dainties with
Poached Cherries and Lemon Sabayon

SERVES 6

120g oats

120g desiccated coconut

1 tbsp ground ginger

100g salted butter

2 tbsp golden syrup

90g light muscovado sugar

Mix the oats, coconut and ginger. Melt the butter, golden syrup and sugar together and cool. Mix with the dry ingredients but do not overwork. Pour into a lightly greased tin measuring about 23 x 23cm – the mixture should be about 2cm deep – and cook for 16 minutes at 160°C/gas mark 2–3. Leave to cool in the tin before cutting into squares of about 4 x 4cm.

Poached Cherries

600g large black cherries

150ml Crème de cassis

Wash the cherries in cold water and remove stalks and stones. Place in a wide saucepan with the crème de cassis, cover with a lid and bring to a boil over a fierce flame. Turn the heat down to a simmer and cook, rolling the cherries around for 3 minutes. Take off the heat , keeping the lid on, and leave to cool for 5 minutes before serving.

Lemon Sabayon

juice and finely grated zest of 2 lemons

12 egg yolks

1 tbsp golden syrup

1 tbsp water

Melt the golden syrup over a low heat with the water, lemon juice and zest. Leave to cool to blood temperature, then add the yolks, whisking furiously until frothy. Put in a double boiler and continue to whisk until the sabayon is cooked. The sabayon should be at the stage of forming ribbons but still light – be careful not to overcook or you will get scrambled eggs.

Make the sabayon at the last minute. Serve in deep plates or soup bowls, placing some warm cherries on a nutty dainty with some sabayon on top.

Warm Chocolate and
Honey Cake with Dried Fruit Salad

SERVES 8

150g extra-bitter chocolate

100ml perfumed clear honey, such as clove or orange blossom

125g powdered hazelnuts

100ml single cream

6 eggs

40g plain white flour

Preheat the oven to 130°C/gas mark 1. Break up the chocolate and melt in a double boiler. Separate the eggs and whisk the yolks with the honey until doubled in volume. Whisk in the melted chocolate, cream and powdered hazelnuts. Finally fold in the flour and stiffly beaten egg whites.

Pour into a buttered 23cm springform cake tin and bake in the oven for 45 minutes. Cool the cake in the tin for 5 minutes before tipping out and serving.

Dried Fruit Salad

16 dried apricots

4 dried figs

200g dried cranberries

100g golden sultanas

200g light muscovado sugar

5 lemons

2 oranges

8 star anise

2 sticks of cinnamon

Peel the oranges and 2 of the lemons and cut the peel into fine julienne strips. Blanch in boiling water and rinse three times. Put the peel in a pan with 100g of sugar, cover with water and bring to the boil. Lower the heat and simmer for 25 minutes until tender. Set aside. Add the remaining sugar to the juice of all the lemons and oranges and bring to the boil.

Mix all the dried fruit and spices in a bowl and pour over the fruit juice and the cooked peel in its syrup. Cover and leave to cool. This can be made a few days in advance, but remember to give the fruit a stir now and then to keep everything moist and submerged.

You can decorate this dessert with dry orange slices. Slice an orange as thinly as possible. Dust the slices with icing sugar and lay them on a non-stick baking sheet. Bake at 80°C/gas mark ¼ for 2 hours or until completely dry

Pastilla of Apple and Prunes with Salted Caramel Sauce

SERVES 4

6 Coxes apples

2 tbsp acacia honey

8 prunes, stoned

4 sheets of brique pastry (North African paper-thin pancakes)

vegetable oil

Preheat the oven to 220°C/gas mark 7. Peel and core the apples, cut them in half and slice thinly. Toss them in the honey and lay on a baking tray. Bake for 10 minutes, then take out and leave to cool. Cut the prunes in half and mix with the cooled apples. Divide this apple and prune mix into 4 and wrap in the brique sheets, sealing the edges with a little water. Brush with vegetable oil and bake at 220°C/gas mark 7 for 8–10 minutes until crisp. Serve with caramel sauce.

Caramel Sauce

1 tbsp salted butter

1 tbsp unrefined caster sugar

120ml single cream

Put the butter and sugar in a pan over a high heat and stir with a wooden spatula until dark brown. Over a low heat, whisk in the single cream and 2 tablespoons of water. Bring back to the boil to dissolve any lumps that may have formed.

Lemon Grass and Citrus 'Consommé' with Raspberries and Lavender Honey Crisps

SERVES 6

2 sticks of lemon grass

1 pink grapefruit

1 orange

1 lime

200g caster sugar

100ml water

Bring the water and sugar to the boil, mixing to keep the sugar from burning. Set aside to cool. Roughly chop the lemon grass. Peel the fruit, removing all the pith, and cut the flesh into large slices. Discard any pips. Put all the ingredients, including the syrup, in a blender and blitz until smooth. Pour into a sieve lined with muslin and set over a bowl. Leave in the refrigerator for 6 hours or until the clear liquid has collected and chilled.

Raspberries and Lavender Crisps

500g raspberries

6 Sheets of brique pastry (North African paper-thin pancakes)

3 tbsp honey

1 tbsp lavender flowers

1 tbsp vegetable oil

Brush the pastry sheets on one side with 1 tablespoon of honey mixed with the oil. Place them on a non-stick baking mat and sprinkle with a few lavender flowers. Cook in a pre-heated oven, 180°C/gas mark 4, for 9–10 minutes until crisp, but not too dark or they will become bitter. Remove from the oven and place the crisps on a cold flat surface.

Arrange the raspberries in bowls, trickle the rest of the honey over them, then pour on the cold consommé. Decorate with lavender flowers and crisps.

Poached Plums In Red Wine
with Toasted Spiced Bread Croutons

SERVES 4

800g plums (you can use a mixture of kinds but make sure they are a similar size)

500ml full-bodied red wine

130g light brown muscovado sugar

4 cinnamon sticks

2 cloves

5 star anise

Wash the plums in cold water. Pour the wine into a wide pan and bring to the boil with the sugar and spices. Add the plums and simmer until the skins start to break and the plums are tender. Roll them around in the wine as they cook to keep them all covered. Cool slightly before serving. This stage can be made in advance and the plums warmed through when needed.

Cut the spiced bread into big cubes, 2 x 2cm. Allow about 5 per person. Put them on a baking sheet and toast under the grill on all sides. Pour the plums and wine into deep plates and scatter over the spiced bread croutons.

Spiced Bread

240g perfumed honey, such as orange blossom or lavender

3 eggs

1 tbsp light muscovado sugar

200g strong dark rye flour

50g strong bread flour

2 tsp baking powder

100ml milk

1 tsp vanilla essence

zest of ½ lemon and ½ orange, finely grated

1 tsp each ground ginger, mixed spice and grated nutmeg

Preheat the oven to 170°C/gas mark 3. Melt the honey and set aside. Whisk the eggs and sugar until frothy, add the honey while still whisking and then the milk. Sift the flours with the baking powder and add to the egg mixture. Finally whisk in the spices, peel and vanilla essence. Pour the mixture into a well-buttered loaf tin lined with silicone paper. Bake for 60–70 minutes. Leave to cool for 15 minutes before taking out of the tin. You can buy good spiced bread (pain d'épices) in delicatessens if you don't want to make your own.

Baked Fruits with Chocolate Sorbet

SERVES 4

4 underripe bananas

1 mango

1 small pineapple

4 fresh purple figs

60g piece of fresh ginger

1 bunch of opal basil

4 cinnamon sticks

100g light muscovado sugar

Peel the bananas, mango and pineapple and cut into bite-size morsels. Cut the figs into quarters. Peel the ginger and slice very thinly, using a knife or a Japanese vegetable slicer. Blanch and rinse the ginger 3 times. Put the blanched ginger in a pan, just cover with water and add the sugar. Bring to a simmer and cook until tender, about 20 minutes.

Preheat the oven to 200°C/gas mark 6. Take four sheets of aluminum foil measuring 30 x 25cm. On each one arrange a mixture of fruit in the centre of the bottom half. Add a cinnamon stick, opal basil leaves and sliced ginger and a drizzling of syrup to each serving. Fold over the aluminum foil and seal the edges by folding over several times. Don't squash the fruit or make the bags too tight. Place them on a baking tray and cook for 15 minutes – the bags should puff up like balloons. Put on to plates and open up just before eating. Serve the chocolate sorbet separately.

Chocolate Sorbet

200ml milk

200ml water

20g cocoa powder

100g caster sugar

50g liquid glucose

160g extra-bitter dark chocolate

Place the milk, water, cocoa powder, sugar and glucose in a saucepan over a high heat and whisk well until boiling. Add the chopped chocolate and bring back to the boil again, whisking well all the time. Pass through a fine sieve and leave to cool before putting into an ice-cream maker.

Warm Spicy Stir-Fried Fruits

A warming pudding for a cold autumn day. Adjust the spicing to your own taste – experiment to find what's right for you.

SERVES 6

6 purple plums
1 pineapple
1 large mango, slightly underripe
2 William pears
6 dried apricots, soaked in water for 20 minutes
1 tsp coriander seeds
1 tsp mustard seeds
1 tsp dry green peppercorns
3 tbsp light muscovado sugar
juice of 3 limes

Peel the pineapple, mango and pears and cut all the fruit into large, bite-size pieces. Crush the coriander seeds and mustard seeds with a pestle and mortar. Heat a wide non-stick pan, add all the spices and cook for 10 seconds to release their aroma. Add the hardest fruit, such as the pears and pineapple, first and stir fry for 30 seconds. Pour in the sugar and, keeping the pan over a high heat, continue adding the softer fruit. Finish with the plums and lime juice. You should end up with fruit that is cooked but still firm, with a dense syrupy sauce. Serve hot with the pineapple crisps for decoration.

Pineapple Crisps

Heat the oven to 130°C/gas mark 1. Slice the pineapple as thinly as possible and place the slices in a single layer on a non-stick baking mat. Sprinkle with icing sugar and put in the oven. They should be dry enough after 20 minutes. Remove the crisps from the mat and place them on a cool, flat surface. As soon as they are cold, store them in an airtight container to keep them crisp.

Lemon Pancake Gâteau

Pancakes

125g unbleached white flour

80g wholemeal flour

2 eggs

a pinch of salt

zest of 2 lemons

500ml milk

vegetable oil

Mix the eggs into the flour with a whisk. Add the milk gradually to avoid any lumps. Finally mix in the salt and lemon zest and leave the batter to rest for 1 hour.

Add a smear of vegetable oil to a non-stick pan and cook the pancakes. This mixture should make about 16. The pancakes should be very thin and well cooked, almost dry.

Lemon Butter

3 eggs

juice and zest of 3 lemons

160g caster sugar

75g butter, cut into small pieces

Whisk the eggs, sugar, lemon juice and zest together in a saucepan. Place over a medium heat and stir continuously until the mixture thickens. Do not boil. Pass through a fine sieve, then whisk in the butter. Cover and leave to cool.

Assembling the dish

Preheat the oven to 200°C/gas mark 6. Line the base of a round, non-stick cake tin, about the same diameter as the pancakes, with greaseproof paper. Place a pancake in the tin followed by a thin layer of the lemon butter. Repeat the layers until all the pancakes and lemon butter have been used. Cover with greaseproof paper and bake in the oven for 20 minutes. Leave to cool in the tin. Cut into slices when cold and serve with fresh berries. Serves 8.

Warm Peaches in Red Wine with Hazelnut Tuiles

SERVES 4

7 yellow peaches
300ml strong red wine
80g dark muscovado sugar
2 tbsp perfumed honey
2 vanilla pods

Split the vanilla pods, scrape out the seeds and mix them with the warmed honey. Put the pods into the red wine with the sugar and boil until the liquid is reduced by half.

Put the peaches into boiling water for 10–15 seconds and refresh in iced water. Peel off the skin and cut each peach into six. Lay 36 of the best slices flat in an ovenproof dish and drizzle with the vanilla honey. Bake at 180°C/gas mark 4 for 10–12 minutes, basting occasionally. The peaches should still be slightly firm.

Put the rest of the peach slices in the red wine and bring to the boil again for 5 minutes, squashing them with the back of a fork. Remove the vanilla pods and blend the mixture until smooth, adding any juices from the baked peaches.

Layer the peaches in between the hazelnut tuiles and pour the red wine sauce around them.

Hazelnut Tuiles

200g ground hazelnuts
150g caster sugar
25g plain flour
140g egg whites (4 or 5)
2 tsp hazelnut oil

Mix the hazelnuts, sugar and flour in a bowl. Do not beat the egg whites but whisk them just enough to break them up. Mix the egg whites and oil into the dry ingredients and leave to rest for at least 30 minutes.

Preheat the oven to 190°C/gas mark 5. Spoon the mixture on to a non-stick baking mat or a lightly greased non-stick tray. Using the back of a spoon, spread each spoonful with a circular motion to make 5cm circles. Bake for 10 minutes or until golden and crisp.

Poached Pears with
Bitter Chocolate Almond Sauce

SERVES 4

4 William pears or similar

500ml water

350g caster sugar

1 vanilla pod, split and seeds scraped out

Put the sugar, scraped vanilla pod and seeds, and water in a pan. Bring to the boil. Peel the pears and remove their cores from the base and place in the simmering syrup. Cover with greaseproof paper. The cooking time depends on the ripeness of the pear – a knife should easily pierce the pear when cooked. Leave the pears in the syrup to cool slightly

Chocolate Almond Sauce

40g extra-bitter chocolate, broken up into pieces

60g unsweetened cocoa powder

120g caster sugar

250ml water

30g unsalted butter

60g almonds, toasted and chopped

Boil the water with the cocoa and sugar, whisking vigorously all the time. Take the pan off the heat and whisk in the butter and chocolate. When the mixture is cool, add the almonds. Serve warm with spiced bread crisps.

Spiced Bread Crisps

Take a loaf of spiced bread (see page 172) and remove the crusts. Slice the loaf as thinly as possible. Lay the slices flat on a baking tray, dust with a little icing sugar and dry in an oven at 130°C/gas mark 1, until crisp. This should take about 30 minutes.

To serve

Put a pear in each bowl, pour over some sauce and top with some spiced bread crisps.

Banana Soufflé with Crumble Topping

SERVES 8

3 bananas

1 tbsp light-brown muscovado sugar

juice of 1 lemon

6 tbsp water

2 tbsp dark rum

1 tbsp cornflour

Peel the bananas and put them in a pan with the sugar, lemon juice and water. Simmer for 5 minutes, squashing the bananas with the back of a fork, then transfer to a food processor and blend until smooth. Dissolve the cornflour in the rum. Return the bananas to the pan and whisk in the cornflour and rum over a heat heat. Bring to the boil, cover and take off the heat.

Compote

4 bananas

juice of 1 lemon

20g demerara sugar

1 tbsp dark rum

Peel and slice the bananas and put them in a pan with the lemon juice, sugar and rum. Cook over moderate heat, mashing with the back of a fork, until cooked and the consistency of compote. Cover and leave to cool.

1 tbsp chopped pistachios and 1 tbsp chopped cashew nuts

1 tbsp rolled oats

1 tbsp demerara sugar

10 egg whites

80g caster sugar

1 tbsp desiccated coconut

icing sugar to dust

Assemble the dish

Preheat the oven to 190°C/gas mark 5. Mix the nuts, coconut, oats and demerara sugar and set aside. Lightly butter 8 ramekins (9cm across x 6cm deep) and dust these with icing sugar. Whisk the egg whites until frothy. Add the caster sugar and continue to whisk until firm. Mix one-third of the egg whites with the banana and cornflour purée until smooth, then lightly fold in the rest of the egg whites. Half fill the ramekins with the egg white mixture. Divide the compote evenly in quenelle shapes between the 8 soufflés, then fill with the rest of the egg white mixture and smooth the surface with a pallet

knife. Run the tip of a knife around the inside of the ramekins to help the soufflés rise evenly. Place the ramekins in the oven and after 4 minutes sprinkle the crumble topping over the soufflés – do this quickly as otherwise the soufflés will fall. Continue to cook for 4–5 minutes. The soufflés should be moist in the middle and slightly undercooked. Serve immediately.

Roast Figs In Vine Leaves

The fig tree grew in the Garden of Eden and its fruit, both dried and fresh, has been popular in the Mediterranean area ever since. Figs are a valuable source of iron, which all athletes need in abundance, but be sure to eat plenty of vitamin C-rich foods at the same time to aid absorption.

SERVES 4

12 fresh purple figs

12–16 fresh vine leaves, depending on size

1 lemon

1 tbsp caster sugar

1 tsp ground ginger

1 tbsp light muscovado sugar

1 tbsp golden sultanas, blanched in boiling water

black pepper

Peel the lemon and cut the peel into julienne strips. Blanch these three times in boiling water, draining and renewing the water each time, then cook them in 160ml of water and 1 tablespoon of caster sugar until translucent. This should take 15–20 minutes. Leave to cool, then add the juice of half the lemon, ground ginger, muscovado sugar, sultanas and a little pepper to taste.

Preheat the oven to 200°C/gas mark 6. Using a sharp knife, cross the figs from the tip to about one-third down. Pinch the figs to open them. To make the parcels, make 4 groups of overlapping vine leaves and put 3 figs on each. Divide the lemon peel and spice mix between the four parcels and then wrap to seal completely and secure with florists' twine. Bake in the preheated oven for 12 minutes. Collect any cooking juices to serve separately. Delicious with a vanilla tapioca sorbet.

Vanilla Tapioca Sorbet

300ml milk
200ml water
125g caster sugar
4 vanilla pods, split and seeds scraped out
2 tbsp tapioca

Add half the sugar to the water and bring to the boil. Add the tapioca and
simmer for 5–6 minutes or until translucent. Leave to cool. Add the rest of
the sugar, vanilla pods and seeds to the milk and bring to the boil. Cover
and leave to cool. Mix both liquids, remove the vanilla pods and pour into an
ice-cream maker.

Cherry Clafoutis

SERVES 6
500g large black cherries, pitted
3 eggs
60g caster sugar
1 vanilla pod, split and seeds scraped out
25g plain flour, sifted
350ml milk
2 tbsp Kirsch

Very lightly butter a quiche or flan dish (23cm x 2.5 cm) and preheat the oven
to 180°C/gas mark 4.

Whisk the eggs and sugar in a bowl until light and pale in colour. Add the
scrapings of the vanilla pod and the sifted flour and slowly pour in the milk
without over-whisking. Pass the mixture through a fine sieve, then pour it into
the dish along with the cherries. Cook for 30 minutes or until puffed up and
set. Douse with the Kirsch and serve warm.

Warm Crunchy Pistachio-Coated Bananas with Honey and Raspberry Coulis

I love honey and use it to sweeten dishes whenever I can. Although it supplies negligible amounts of nutrients and energy in the form of simple carbohydrates, I prefer its versatility to plain sugar. Honey's medicinal properties are well known and there is nothing quite like a hot toddy made with dark rum, lemon and honey to soothe a sore throat and encourage a good night's sleep. Until the early 1600s, honey was used as a sweetener – sugar was only for the gentry and those who could afford it. By the late 1600s the opposite was true and honey was fast becoming a luxury, hence the line in the nursery rhyme, 'the queen was in her parlour eating bread and honey'.

SERVES 4

4 ripe bananas

180g peeled pistachios

1 tbsp icing sugar

480g raspberries

4 tbsp clear flower-scented honey

Roughly chop the pistachios and place them on a large plate. Peel the bananas and cut them in half. Roll the banana halves in the nuts, making sure they are evenly coated by slightly pressing them into the nuts. Dust with some icing sugar and place on a non-stick baking mat. Bake at 200°C/gas mark 6 for 4–5 minutes, until just tender and warm – no longer or the bananas will completely melt. Keep warm.

To make the raspberry coulis, blend half the raspberries with two tablespoons of honey until smooth. Pass the mixture through a fine sieve to remove the pips.

Divide the bananas on to 4 warm plates and drizzle with the rest of the honey. Serve with some raspberries in a neat pyramid and some raspberry coulis on the side.

Chocolate-Dipped Fruits

There's a large amount of chocolate in this recipe, but you need plenty in order to dip the fruit properly.

SERVES 6

12 strawberries

3 seedless clementines

18 physalis (Cape gooseberries)

12 cherries

3 fresh figs

800g extra-bitter chocolate, 70 per cent cocoa solids

4 tbsp desiccated coconut

Wash and dry the strawberries. Carefully peel the clementines, making sure not to break the delicate membrane of each segment. Cut the figs into quarters and pull back the leaves of the Cape gooseberries. Put the coconut on to a plate.

Melt the chocolate over a pan of warm water, stirring frequently. Do not let the chocolate go over 50°C. Take the pan off the heat and stir well with a spatula. Dip the pieces of fruit, one by one, into the chocolate, shaking off any excess chocolate, then place the fruit in the desiccated coconut.

Refrigerate for 15 minutes to set the chocolate and keep in a cool place until needed. Keep any left-over chocolate for another recipe.

'I love chocolate – but only the best. I don't see the point of eating cheap confectionery.'

Index

Acknowledgements

Thank you to the following people: John Brookes from VICTA charity for which I raise money. A tireless man, he is always prepared to listen to my woes and has frequently given me encouragement when needed.

Marion Oputa, who once again has managed to decipher my scribbled lines and often stayed late to complete the task so that Susan Haynes, David Rowley, Jinny Johnson and Clive Hayball from Weidenfeld and Nicolson could bring this book together.

Nicolas Laridan, Bryn Williams and Monica Faafiti from the kitchen of Le Gavroche for cooking the food for the photos as I was on crutches due to an untimely broken leg.

Tara Fisher who captured the feel of this book through her photography despite being heavily pregnant.

Finally to my wife Gisele for washing the smelly sweaty training kit and Emily my daughter for the occasional foot massage.

Notes Eggs and milk: use large, free-range, organic eggs and whole milk. Herbs: a bunch means an average supermarket pack – usually about 25g. Pepper: use freshly ground black pepper unless otherwise specified. Baking mat: this is a non-stick mat made of heatproof silicon, available from good kitchen suppliers. It doesn't have to be greased and can be placed on a baking tray or straight on to the oven rack.

First published in the United Kingdom in 2003 by Weidenfeld & Nicolson an imprint of the Orion Publishing Group

This paperback edition first published in 2004 by Seven Dials Paperbacks
Weidenfeld & Nicolson
Wellington House
125 Strand
London WC2 0BB

Text copyright © Michel Roux Jr 2003
Design and layout copyright © Weidenfeld & Nicolson 2003

Michel Roux Jr has asserted his right to be identified as the author of this Work in accordance with the Copyright, Designs and Patents Act of 1988.

Copyright Licensing Agency, 90 Tottenham Court Road, London W1P 9HE. Applications for the copyright owner's written permission to reproduce any part of this publication should be addressed to the publisher.

A CIP catalogue record for this book is available from the British Library

ISBN 1 84188 235 6

Design director David Rowley
Editorial director Susan Haynes
Designed by Clive Hayball
Edited by Jinny Johnson
Proofread by Gwen Rigby
Index by Valerie Chandler

Photographs by Tara Fisher